TRUE

True Happiness

D. Martyn Lloyd-Jones

Gwasg Bryntirion Press

Unless otherwise stated, Scripture quotations are from the
Authorised (King James) Version

*Cover desig*n: burgum boorman ltd.

Published by
Gwasg **Bryntirion** Press
Bryntirion, Bridgend CF31 4DX, Wales UK
Printed by WBC Book Manufacturers, Bridgend

Contents

1
The search for happiness

*Blessed is the man that walketh not in the counsel
of the ungodly, nor standeth in the way of sinners, nor
sitteth in the seat of the scornful. But his delight is in the law
of the Lord; and in his law doth he meditate day and night.*
(Psalm 1:1-2)

This first psalm is very interesting and the authorities are agreed that it has a very real significance. It is undoubtedly a kind of general introduction to the whole of the Book of Psalms. This is a book that teaches a definite philosophy, a view of life. You find it also in Proverbs and in the other wisdom literature (Job, Ecclesiastes); you find it also in the more didactic portions, the theological portions of the Bible. But here it is, in this particular poetic form, expressed as an experience through which the writer, the Psalmist, has passed; how he has understood the teaching of God with respect to that, and how God, in that very experience, has led him into a yet further and deeper understanding of his ways with respect to men. So this psalm is an introduction and, therefore, we can find in it—as we might expect—the basic teaching and philosophy of the entire book.

One message

But it is, at the same time, therefore, and for the reason I have just been giving, a very good introduction to and summary of the message of the entire Bible. For the Bible has only one message in it: it puts it in a variety of ways, but it is only one message. There is quite a lot of geography and geology, a great deal of history; a great deal about kings, princes, wars, fightings, births, marriages, deaths; endless details, but only one theme; it is men and women in their relationship to God and what God has done about us and our salvation.

So you get this brought out in every part and portion of the Bible, and, as it is the great theme of the Book of Psalms as a whole, so, in particular, it is concentrated here in this first psalm. We are entitled to say, therefore, that we have here a kind of distillation of the essential teaching of the Bible with respect to men and women and their lives in this world and in time. That is why I am calling your attention to it.

We are creatures of time, and that is why new years* and old years make a difference to us. We divide time up in this way: there is nothing wrong in that if we use it correctly. Anything that makes us stop and consider and pause and meditate; anything that makes us look into these matters and consider our whole relationship to Almighty God is a good thing.

'But', someone may say, 'why do you do this? Aren't you a bit behind the times? Aren't you a sort of anachronism in this modern world? Can't you give us something up-to-date? Can't you give us something modern? Can't you give us some new teaching? We are in a new world, the scientific age. Can't you trace life as it is today and give us the essence of your understanding and your meditation upon it and what others are thinking and advocating? Why don't you try to look into the future and forecast what's going to happen? Why don't you tell us what we ought to be doing, what we

---

* This sermon was preached on the first Sunday of 1963.

ought to be agitating about, and trying to get our statesmen to do? Why don't you try to draw up some plan for world order or a better way of living? Why don't you do something like that: why do you go back to that old Book of yours? Why don't you do something new?'

That, I feel, is a fair question. I do not object to it. And the answer to it is given in a book of the Bible called Ecclesiastes: 'There is no new thing under the sun' (Eccles. 1:9). Nothing at all: nothing new! If somebody could demonstrate to me that the conditions in which we find ourselves in the world today are really different, then I would think there was something in the argument which demands a new approach, but I think I shall be able to show you that there is nothing different at all.

The condition of men and women in this world is still what it has always been. You notice what people were looking for in the time of the Psalmist. Happiness. 'Happy is the man'—that is it!—'happy is the man that walketh not in the counsel of the ungodly.' Blessed—happy. They were looking for happiness, and this man knew that; he had been looking for it himself.

So the fundamental need of people today is still happiness. We are not the first people that have wanted to be happy; humanity has always been looking for this. The whole story of life, history and civilisation has been nothing but this great quest for happiness. Nobody wants to be miserable; nobody wants to be unhappy; everybody is looking for joy and happiness and rejoicing. So the conditions are exactly the same, there is nothing new.

'Ah, but', you say, 'look at the world.' But the world has always been as it is; a place of war and jealousy; a place of envy, malice, spite and disappointment. It has always been like that. It may take different forms, but that does not make any difference to the thing in and of itself; a cannon at one time used to be quite as terrifying as the bomb is to us. It is simply the form that has changed; the essential conditions, the precarious state of life in this world is not something new. There is no new thing under the sun. So there is no need to leave this old teaching, because it faces the same problem.

But I have a much higher reason than that for calling your attention to it, and it is that this is God's teaching; all else is man's teaching. Oh, I know that the philosophers have investigated this problem of happiness; some of them have written their Utopias. That is what it was all about: seeking for happiness, for blessedness. But, you see, it has all come to nothing. Here we have God's prescription for happiness. God's! That is why I go back to the Bible. It is because this book is essentially and altogether different from every other book. It is not a human book; not a human production; not a human invention; not a category and a list of human thoughts. It is God's revelation. It always has been and it still is. And this is what the world needs today as much as it has ever needed it—indeed, even more so.

But let me add a further reason. Here is a teaching that is confirmed by the experience of the ages. Here is a book which puts it as Psalm 37 puts it: 'I have been young and now am old' (v.25): a man speaking out of his experience. So you get here the experience of individuals, the experience of nations, and it is a very good thing to look back across a span of history. We think we know so much, we are so clever and we are so different. But the more you look back and read history, the more, again, will you find that there is indeed nothing new under the sun.

Men and women have always been in this present predicament and have always been seeking for the happiness that eludes them. Is it not a good thing, therefore, to look back across this record in which people and nations will tell us of the false way and the true way; the record of those who say, 'At last I've found it; this is it!'? That is what you find here; the man who believed God's instruction and had put it into practice. That is another reason for going back.

And then, finally, it is a book that confronts us, and brings plainly and clearly before us the great fundamental choice. Now that leads me to make a remark or two about the whole biblical method of facing the problem of life. The thing that differentiates the Bible from every other book and every other teaching, the glory of this, is that it is essentially simple. I do not know if you have ever tried reading these books on philosophy? I find them very difficult! With their involved terminology, who can follow them? Thank God, here is a book that is simple, direct and plain; a book that reduces the complexity of the problem to just one big thing. The Bible always puts it like this. It says, 'You are confronted by two alternatives: and there are only two'; it says that from the beginning to the end. Only two alternatives: the way of God and the way of Satan; the way of Abel and the way of Cain; the way of Jacob and the way of Esau. Here in this psalm is a man who is a good man, he is a godly man, a righteous man. And then there is the ungodly, the wicked. It is always these alternatives.

So the Bible is a unique book that puts it simply and directly, and reduces all the complexities to just this one thing: which way am I going? It is either this or that. And, of course, it goes further. It helps me by putting it in the form of illustrations, and that is what we have in this psalm.

Oh, if we but realised God's heart of love! He wants us to know, to understand; he stoops to our weakness; he condescends to our ignorance. He uses pictures, illustrations, history—anything, to bring the truth home to us. And this is what he is doing here. We are shown two men, the ungodly and the righteous. We have a wrong way and a right way, a bad way and a good way; we have a negative way and a positive way. And that is the essence of good teaching: that the matter is not only put before us positively, but also negatively, in order that we may see the contrast and be helped by the illustrations.

What is the teaching, therefore? Well, we are, as we have seen, anxious to be happy. 'Oh, the blessedness', says the Psalmist, 'the blessedness of this righteous man'. Yes, but the question is, How has he acquired it? How does he arrive at this? And this is the Bible's teaching with respect to that most vital matter of all. You want to be happy, do you not? You would like to be able to think that you will be blessed in spite of what may happen to you?

And it is possible! This is the Bible's teaching, and, trying to emulate the example of the Bible and its teachers, in order to make it simple, I have also tried to divide up this matter into theory and practice. That is always the right way of approach. First, you look at the theory of the thing, then at what it actually tells you to do. And that is exactly what we are given here in these two verses.

First, then, the theory, which is most important. Never believe anyone who tells you that you do not need it, that you just plunge into the practice of something. No, if you are wise you will read about it first and understand a little about the theory before you begin to act upon it. So the first thing the Bible tells us is that happiness is possible. And I emphasise that because this is the most staggering, the most surprising thing of all in a world like this; but it is the great message of the Bible. It comes to us as we are, and it says, 'Happiness, blessedness is possible.'

Now many start out in life thinking that they can easily find happiness and keep it. They think that they have some secret that nobody has ever had before. 'Those middle-aged people', we say when we are young, 'and those old people, they've gone astray of course. Fools, they don't understand; look at them—back numbers! We know, we've got the secret, we are going to find it.' We start out like that. But it is not being pessimistic, it is just being true to facts to say that we have not gone very far before we begin to suspect that it is not as easy as we thought, and we soon find that if there is anything that is utterly elusive in this world, it is happiness.

What is the next stage? Well, the ultimate stage with most people—indeed with all people unless they become Christians—is that they fall perhaps into despair and into an utter sense of hopelessness. 'Peace, perfect peace, in this dark world of sin?' says the hymn-writer—'Impossible! Utterly impossible', they say.

There are many in that condition and, whether we like it or not, it is just a fact that the greatest literature in the world happens to be tragic literature. Shakespeare's greatest plays are his tragedies. The greatest pieces of literature that came out of Greece are the Greek tragedies. Why? Because life is tragic. That is where the Peter Pan, butterfly idea of life is just nonsense. Everything that is great and big in life is always proclaimed—as a Spanish writer once described it— as 'the tragic sense of life'.

Life is a tragedy. It appears everywhere; it is all around us, and this is the great problem and the quest of human beings; they are seeking for happiness, because they find themselves in the midst of tragedy. But so many come to the conclusion that it is impossible, when the only outcome is that often depicted so brilliantly by Shakespeare—the last scene with almost everybody being killed. That is the end of it all—tragedy!

13

But others go beyond that. They are not only filled with despair and an utter sense of hopelessness, they have become cynical. 'Life,' they say, 'what is it?' Shakespeare again, knowing all kinds and types of humanity, has put it into the mouth of one of them: he says, What is life? It is nothing but 'A tale told by an idiot, full of sound and fury, signifying— *nothing*!' That is cynicism. That is life, 'A tale told by an idiot.' And when you read the history of the human race you cannot help feeling that there is something in that. What are these wars and all the preparations for wars, but sheer idiocy, lunacy, madness! Man is an idiot, he is a fool.

The cynic has come to see that, and he says so. Some of the poets also have expressed this view; here is one of them, a typical cynic:

> I strove with none, for none was worth my strife;
>> Nature I loved, and next to Nature, Art.
> I warmed both hands before the fire of life;
>> It sinks, and I am ready to depart.
>>>> Walter Savage Landor

That is the blasé attitude of so many today. Another man has put it like this:

> Since ev'ry man who lives is born to die,
> And none can boast sincere felicity,
> With equal mind, what happens let us bear
> Nor joy nor grieve too much for things beyond our care.
> Like pilgrims to th' appointed place we tend:
> The world's an inn, and death the journey's end.
>>>> John Dryden

'Very well,' he says, 'don't be too happy, don't be too miserable; just go through it as best you can, not crying over spilt milk, not hoping for anything.' 'No matter where you are or what you are doing,' says the cynic, 'there's always a fly in the ointment.' 'Vanity of vanities, all is vanity' (Eccles. 1:2). That is the conclusion the intelligent world comes to. The moment you get a thinker in the world who is not a Christian, he comes to one or the other of those conclusions. He either sinks down in despair or he sits in the corner in his cynicism and speaks thus about life.

The Bible answers all that and denies it. It says, 'Yes, what you've been saying is true in a sense—but . . . you've left out the most important factor: *God*! 'Blessed is the man . . .' Happiness is possible even in this world. 'Peace, perfect peace, in this dark world of sin?'—Yes. 'The blood of Jesus whispers peace within.' This is a great protest against the despair, the hopelessness, the cynicism of a world without God. That is the first thing I find in the theory here in Psalm 1.

But, secondly, the Bible, once more, is unique and different from everything else, in that it tells us, here at the very outset, that we do not find happiness because we seek it in the wrong way. That is where theory comes in. Most people say, 'I'm out for happiness!' and off they go. My friends, sit down, wait for a moment, look at the theory. You must learn how to look for happiness, because if you do not look for it in the right way you will never arrive. If you start on the wrong road you will arrive at the wrong destination. It is as simple as that, so you must be right in your theory, and the Bible has its theory with regard to the secret of how happiness is to be found.

Some important negatives

The *first* negative is that happiness does not depend, ultimately, upon circumstances. Is that not important? We all think, do we not, that our happiness depends upon

15

circumstances? Pockets full of money, sun shining, all's well. But if I lose my money or if circumstances go against me, how can I be happy? Human happiness depends upon circumstances and events and happenings, and as you look forward into the future, no doubt you have said to yourself, 'If this happens, how wonderful it's going to be! If it doesn't happen, then chaos is come again, and I never can and never shall be happy.' Oh, but how wrong that is! This is the first principle of the biblical teaching: happiness does not depend at all upon those things.

The *second* negative—and here is the great wisdom of the Bible—is that happiness must never be sought as an end in and of itself. It is a by-product of something else. 'Blessed is the man that seeketh after blessedness'? No! 'Blessed is the man that walketh not in the counsel of the ungodly . . . but his delight is in the law of the Lord, and in his law doth he meditate day and night.' He is not seeking happiness. This is the essence of wisdom. If you seek happiness and live for it, you will never get it; never!

That is the great message here, but let me give it in its New Testament form. Listen to our Lord: 'Blessed are they who hunger and thirst after righteousness, for they shall be filled.' Not blessed are they that hunger and thirst after happiness, but 'Blessed [happy] are they which do hunger and thirst after *righteousness*, for they shall be filled' (Matt. 5:6). It is not the people who seek this elusive happiness, but the people who seek righteousness, who will find it.

Again, look how he put it later on in that same Sermon on the Mount: 'Look,' he says in effect, 'you are making an awful mistake. You are saying, "What shall we eat, what shall we drink, or wherewithal shall we be clothed? My happiness depends upon food and drink and clothing. And what's going to happen to me?" Oh the tragedy of your blindness!', says our Lord; 'Seek ye first the kingdom of God and his righteousness, and all these [other] things shall be added unto you' (Matt. 6:31,33).

They are thrown into the bargain. If you seek happiness, you will never find it; it will always elude you, it will always escape you. You will think you have got it, but suddenly it is gone; it is like trying to catch an iridescent bubble—the moment you catch it it has vanished, broken in your hands, there is nothing left. 'No, no, that's the whole mistake,' says the Bible, 'get your theory right. Never make happiness an end in and of itself. It is always an indirect result. It is always a by-product of something infinitely greater.' To put it positively: 'Happiness', says the Bible, 'depends upon two things only. One: our relationship to God and his righteousness. Two: it depends upon what I am, not upon what is happening to me. That is the secret.'

Oh, what a profound book this is! Why do people not listen to it? There is a statement by Shakespeare which I am never tired of quoting, it puts it so perfectly:

> The fault, dear Brutus, is not in our stars,
> But in ourselves, that we are underlings.

It is you yourself, not what happens to you. 'Two men looked out through prison bars; The one saw mud, the other stars.' The circumstances may be identical, but, oh, the difference in the two men! And that difference was in the men, not in their surroundings.

> A primrose by a river's brim
> A yellow primrose was to him,
> And it was nothing more.
> William Wordsworth

That was one sort of man; but here is another:

17

To me the meanest flower that blows can give
Thoughts that do often lie too deep for tears.

William Wordsworth

'Beauty is in the eye of the beholder.' It is not circumstances, it is not events that will determine whether you will
be happy or not; it is your relationship to God, it is what you
yourself are. That, then is the theory.

So we move on to the practice, and, again, it is as simple
and plain, and as explicit, as anything can be. If any of us
ever arrives in hell we will have nobody to blame but ourselves. You will never be able to say that the message was so
difficult and complicated that you could not follow it. Is this
not the ABC? Is it not essentially simple? The Psalmist does
not stop at the theory; he works it out in detail because he
knows us so well.

What, then, is the practice? 'Blessed', he says, 'is the man
that walketh *not* . . .' Here, again, it starts with a negative. We
do not like negatives, do we? We are much too intelligent;
we do not need to be told what not to do! What we want is to
be told what to do. Is that not the modern attitude? The Bible
is always saying, 'Thou shalt not . . . Thou shalt not . . .' Of
course it is! Why?

Starting with the negative

Well, it is most important, as one faces life, to understand
why the negative comes before the positive, and here are the
reasons for that. *First*, the Bible starts with the negative
because it is the most realistic book in the whole world. It
starts, always, with the world as it is. But we do not like that;
we start by painting pretty pictures! Here we are setting out
in life: 'Now then,' we say, 'we are going to be happy'; so we
paint a wonderful picture; we begin to dream, and that is
why we never find happiness! You must start by being a

realist; you must start with the world as it is and where it is. I know that that is most uncomfortable and one does not like to do it.

I am reminded here of the story of the Irishman. A traveller in Ireland once stopped a man working at the roadside and said, 'Now, my friend, if you were going to Dublin which way would you go?' The answer from the Irishman was this: 'I wouldn't go from here.' There is a very profound lesson in that, is there not? But we are all Irishmen in a spiritual sense. 'How do you go?' 'I wouldn't go from here.' Exactly! In other words you do not want to face yourself. You want to start somewhere else. You want to make a leap of a thousand miles, then you would have a start in your chartered aeroplane to happiness. But, my dear friend, you are where you are, and you must start from there whether you like it or not. That is realism. And the Bible never evades the facts; it makes us face them with a stark reality that nothing else in the world does. It is a most honest book.

Secondly, the Bible always starts with a negative condemnation because the first thing it has to tell us is that life as it is in this world is evil. There is no hope for men and women until they are convicted of sin. The first thing they must get hold of is that as they are, they are wrong, and their whole world is wrong and evil and vile. 'Blessed is the man that walketh not . . .' It shouts it at us and it pulls us up and we need that. 'Isn't life wonderful?', says the world. 'No,' says the Bible, 'it's foul and ugly.'

Thirdly, the Bible always starts with a negative, because if you want to be a good physician of the soul—or of anything else—you had better start with making a diagnosis before you rush after treatment. You must spend a little time in investigating the case before you apply some soothing syrup. But we do not like that. We say, 'Give us something different; give us something that will ease the pain; give us something that will make us feel happy.' No, no, if you are a good physician, you say, 'Now what is the cause of this man's trouble? I must investigate, I must examine.' You must take his history, you must pummel him, you must delve into the depths until you know the cause of his trouble. But if you start treating him without discovering the cause, then you are a criminal physician. But that is what the whole world is doing. It never likes to make a diagnosis. It says, 'Come with me; I'll give you a show, I'll put something before you. You've never seen anything so wonderful in all your life!' And at once the world can give you in a package everything you want. But it cannot. You must start with diagnosis and with discovering the cause. So you deal with the problem like this: you ask, 'If you say you want to be happy, then the first question is, why are you unhappy?' It is common sense, is it not?

Fourthly, the first steps to salvation, always, are recognition of the evil of sin and the need for repentance. Repent and believe the gospel. John the Baptist always precedes the Lord Jesus Christ. Conviction of sin always comes before pardon and forgiveness. No one will find happiness until he has turned away from evil finally, and has committed himself to God.

Next—and this is the most important of all—let me put the fifth and sixth points in one in order to emphasise it. The Bible hurls a negative at us at the very beginning like this in order to tell us that God's way of life and of salvation is entirely and essentially different from all we have ever known. The Bible says, 'The way of happiness is *not* what you and all others have always fondly thought it is. If you come and listen to me,' says the Bible, 'you've got to be prepared for a surprise. You've got to be prepared to hear something you've never heard in your life before. Something you've never imagined even; something that is revolutionary, something that comes from another world.' Precisely! This is not man, this is God. This is not of earth, it is heaven coming down. This is eternity coming into time. It is altogether different. The way to blessedness is *not* . . . it is a 'no' to everything in which we have ever believed and trusted. It is going to be something that humanity has never thought of even at the very height of its powers and abilities. It is God's way, and it is unique.

Details

That, then, is the explanation of the negatives, so we come now to the actual details. They are quite simple. What must I avoid? Well, *first*, 'the counsel of the ungodly'. 'Blessed is the man that walketh not in the counsel of the ungodly', which means that if you want to be happy, the first thing you must do is to stop listening to the whole outlook of the world at the present time; that outlook which is without God and opposed to God, and which does not recognise him.

That is why the world is as it is; it is because it is ungodly. 'God is not in all his thoughts', says the Psalmist in another place about this same sort of evil man (Ps. 10:4). 'If you want to be happy,' says the Bible, 'don't walk in the *counsels* of the ungodly', and 'counsels' there means those things that the ungodly man advises you to do. He says, 'Don't waste your time going to those churches; don't waste your time in reading that old book called the Bible. It's out of date; exploded; science has knocked it into a cocked hat! There's nothing there at all. Don't believe in God: believe in yourself!'

Ungodly: that is his counsel. He trusts his own wisdom; he trusts his own understanding; he trusts his own knowledge, though he has to admit that what was believed as science fifty years ago is now laughed at—as has happened throughout the centuries. And undoubtedly what is believed now will be laughed at in fifty years time. But he still trusts it: he trusts his own reason, his own investigations and discoveries; he trusts himself and his own innate powers, and he dismisses God and everything that God represents. There is the ungodly person.

But the word that is translated here as 'ungodly' is a very interesting one. In the very word that is used, there is a sense of restlessness. And the ungodly must be restless because he does not know; his knowledge is contingent; he is always having to change his theories because something is discovered which disproves them. I am old enough to remember that. I was taught that the atom was indivisible, it was the smallest particle of matter. The atom: the ultimate small thing! And that certainty? It has gone, it has been completely exploded. 'Very well', says the Bible, 'don't walk in the counsels of such a man. Don't listen to him!'

Secondly, do not 'stand in the way of sinners'. There is no need to explain this: if you want to be happy, you must avoid the way of the world, the way of the sinner. He lives to his flesh. He lives to eat and to drink and to indulge in sex. Now, I am not here to preach against these things, I am just here to tell you that you will never find happiness that way. Nobody ever has. They think they have; they soon find they have not. Do not stand in the way of sinners: it will never give you happiness.

And, then, *thirdly*, do not 'sit in the seat of the scorners'. Who are these? They are the scoffers, the people who stick out their tongues at everything that is sacred and holy and sanctified. These are the clever people who laugh at religion and joke at it, who scoff at God, at his law and at his ordinances; who scoff at all the sanctities in life, marriage and everything else. These are the people who scoff at morality and decency, and they call it 'self-expression'.

These are the popular people today who make fun of everything; nothing is sacred, nothing is to be admired, everything is to be laughed at and joked about—God included. How clever it is, how facile; praised by the critics! The seat of the scorners, the scoffers, the mere clever manipulators, the soul-less men and women who know nothing about the glories of life. The empty people who live on their wits and have nothing but wits; nothing precious; nothing tender; nothing beautiful; nothing clean; nothing worth dying for; nothing at all.

Now that is what the Psalmist tells us in detail: 'Blessed is the man that walketh not in the counsel of the ungodly, nor standeth in the way of sinners, nor sitteth in the seat of the scornful.' Is there a progression here? I believe there is. Walking, standing, sitting. It is a wonderful picture of the increasing grip that sin has on us all, the increasing grip that bad practices and evil habits have upon the soul. At first you walk with it; you say, 'Oh, I'm not going to be a slave to this: I'm walking, I'm still moving!' Yes, but a stage will soon come when you will be standing and no longer walking. And then a stage will come when you will be sitting. It will have you in its grip, and there you will be—seated.

But there is another aspect to this progression and that is the increasing paralysis that is produced by sin; how it causes a man or woman, and the finest things in them, always to degenerate, so that, finally, there they are sitting in the corner and saying, 'What is the use of anything? Let us eat, drink, and be merry for tomorrow we die.' 'Sitting in the seat of the scorners.' What a description! There they are, useless and motionless; they do nothing, they affect nothing, they just sit and mutter and splutter out their cleverness. Scoffers and scorners. Do not listen to them. They are about as far removed from happiness as anyone can be. They have lost everything and they have no hope at all; they just sit paralysed by evil and by sin.

The secret of happiness

There, then, is the negative. Let me just give you the positive briefly. It is simply the outworking of the theory I gave you at the beginning. Here is the secret of happiness. It is that a man or woman 'delights in the law of the Lord', not in the cleverness of the philosophers or the speculations of the so-called thinkers; not in following the ungodly with their own meditations and cogitations; but the law of the Lord—the Bible; God's rule; Old Testament and New; the law and the gospel. Here it is, everything I need. God's way to happiness; it is all here before me.

And those who are blessed delight in it, you notice. They do not merely take an intellectual interest in it. They do not read it merely because they are afraid of not doing so, and afraid of the consequences of sin. They do not look into it simply because they are utilitarians and think that it may help them. 'Honesty is the best policy and I want to get on, so I don't do certain things for that reason.' That is not their attitude. They *delight* in the law of the Lord. They have great pleasure in knowing it. They say, 'Isn't it wonderful?' They 'meditate in it day and night' because, they say, 'there's nothing like it. Everything else is vain, a sham, a will o' the wisp. Here it is! God's truth, God's wisdom, and—how marvellous!—it works, it gives me what I want.' They enjoy it. This is the happy man, the happy woman.

Let me put it to you as the Psalmist himself puts it. Our translation is not quite as good as it might be. I read here:

'Blessed is the man', but what the Psalmist wrote was this: 'O the blessedness of the man!' Why? To bring out the fulness, the variety, the largeness, the Psalmist says, 'I can't describe it. O the blessedness . . . How wonderful it is!' Listen to John Newton trying to reduce all that to verse:

> See! the streams of living waters,
>   Springing from eternal love,
> Well supply thy sons and daughters,
>   And all fear of want remove:
> Who can faint while such a river
>   Ever flows their thirst to assuage—
> Grace which, like the Lord the Giver,
>   Never fails from age to age?

It is the blessedness of the knowledge of sins forgiven; the blessedness of knowing that everything that I did and said and thought in the past, that was unclean and unworthy and sinful, has been blotted out by God in his love, because Christ died for me. Oh, the blessedness of knowing that the past has been forgotten and will never be brought against me again! Forgiveness and pardon.

What else? Well, life in Christ. Life in God. Our Lord said, 'I am come that they might have life, and that they might have it more abundantly' (John 10:10). That is it; the blessedness of receiving life from God, and peace and joy, and this abundance, this fulness. They shall go in and out and find pasture (John 10:9); there will never be an end.

> Plenteous grace with Thee is found,
>   Grace to cover all my sin;
> Let the healing streams abound,
>   Make and keep me pure within.
> Thou of life the fountain art,
>   Freely let me take of Thee;

> Spring Thou up within my heart,
> Rise to all eternity.
>
> Charles Wesley

Have you got this blessedness? Do you know this happiness? Do you delight in the Bible? Do you delight in God? Do you delight in the Lord Jesus Christ? Do you delight in meditating about the joys and the glories of eternity? If you do, it does not matter what the world does to you, you will continue to be blessed; you will continue to be happy; nothing can ever take it from you, it is in you, it is between you and God and independent of circumstances.

How can you get this? You cannot *make* yourself enjoy the Bible. You try doing it and you will find that it does not work. You cannot make yourself a righteous and a good person: your will is too weak. Do not put the slightest faith in your New Year's resolutions; they will soon have gone. There is only one way to get this blessedness. Come to the Bible and it will meet you and say to you, 'Now listen; you are unhappy and miserable because you've been living the life of the world, of men and women in sin. You must come out of that.' But how can you? Do as you will, you will never extricate yourself.

'No', says the Bible, 'but God so loved the world, that he gave his only begotten Son, that whosoever believeth in him should not perish, but have everlasting life' (John 3:16). 'The Son of man is come to seek and to save that which was lost' (Luke 19:10). Listen to this instruction, this law of the Lord, and it will tell you, Repent and believe the gospel. Acknowledge your sin; acknowledge your failure; believe that Jesus of Nazareth is the Son of God and that he came into this world and died on the cross to bear the punishment of your sin, to set you free, to reconcile you to God, to give you new life, and to make you an heir of eternal bliss.

Believe it!—and you will find that he has put new life into you. You will become a new being. You will find that you really do enjoy the Bible, you will 'delight in the law of the Lord'. You will want to read it more than anything else, and you will lose your taste for the world and its fading pleasures. And you will want to know more about God and about Christ and about the hope of glory.

> Saviour, if of Zion's city
> I, through grace, a member am,
> Let the world deride or pity,
> I will glory in Thy Name.
> Fading is the worldling's pleasure,
> All his boasted pomp and show;
> Solid joys and lasting treasure,
> None but Zion's children know.
>
> John Newton

Do you know them? Listen to this wisdom. This is the way, the only way; forsake the ungodly, his thought, his practice, his everything. Believe the message of God in Christ. Receive it into your heart. Give yourself to him and ask him to fill you with this new life which alone can make us blessed, and keep us blessed, whatever may happen to us in this world of time.

2
The chaff

*And he shall be like a tree planted by the
rivers of water, that bringeth forth his fruit
in his season; his leaf also shall not wither; and
whatsoever he doeth shall prosper. The ungodly
are not so: but are like the chaff which
the wind driveth away.*
(Psalm 1:3-4)

There is one thing that brings the whole of humanity to a common denominator; and that is the desire to be happy. Some people have strange ways of showing that desire, but they all have it.

A universal book

The Bible claims that it is a universal book for that reason. It is the textbook of life, the manual of the soul. It is *the* book that deals with men and women and their whole state and condition as they pass through this world of time, and so, as I have said, I make no apology for calling your attention to this old problem of humanity and of happiness in terms of the Bible, or in terms of this first psalm. For until mankind has discovered happiness apart from this, I will go on preaching it. And that means that I will go on until I die, and others will go on after I have gone, because, according to the Bible, men and women will never find happiness apart from the way that is indicated here.

So it is a perennial truth. It is always a contemporary message. The Bible never dates; it is the most up-to-date book in the world today. All the other teachings and philosophies are constantly being put on the scrap-heap; what do you think of the science or the philosophy of fifty years ago? It is all now ridiculed, laughed at, thrown into the limbo of things long-since forgotten.

But here is a message that is still contemporary, and the reason for that, as we saw earlier, is that it is indeed the word of God, and the man or woman who finds happiness is the one who delights in the law of the Lord and who meditates in it day and night. The case put forward here in the psalm, as we also saw, is that people are not happy and they do not find happiness because they always seek it in the wrong way.

They always make the mistake of approaching it directly. They have never yet learned that in the spiritual realm, as in the military realm, the best strategy is what is generally called the strategy of 'the indirect approach'. It is always true in the Bible; if you seek righteousness, you will get happiness; but if you seek happiness, you will not get it.

And we saw, too, that the second big mistake that people make is that they persistently think that happiness is something that is constantly dependent upon circumstances. That is a great fallacy because, if happiness were dependent upon that, then there would never be such a thing as happiness in this world. But we are told here that there is—'Blessed is the man . . .'—and it is a happiness that is independent of circumstances. Furthermore, we are told that it is something that is ultimately dependent upon our relationship to God and the state and the condition of our own souls. It is a happiness that is true and, because it is true, it is something that lasts and continues and abides whatever may chance to come across our path.

So this is the great question: Why do people not believe this and then go on to experience this blessedness, this happiness, that the Bible talks about? And there are two main explanations of that.

The *first* is that men and women are so terribly ignorant about themselves; they do not see themselves as they really are. Because of that, they start on a false assumption, the assumption that they themselves are all right and that the trouble is somebody or something else. So they have already gone wrong, and while they are wrong like this at the very beginning, they cannot, of course, hope ever to arrive at true happiness. They must learn the truth about themselves, and they will never learn that unless they believe in this 'law of the Lord', this message which we have in the Bible.

There is nothing under the heavens that tells us the truth about ourselves save this book. But here are men and women reading newspapers, and they will never find the truth about themselves there, because though, in a sense, the newspapers are telling the truth about them, it is put in a form which they are pleased with. People enjoy it and are entertained by it instead of being convicted by it. But anyone who reads a newspaper today should have a terrible feeling of conviction. As we read about the nations piling up armaments; as we read about disputes within our own country, we should all be heartily ashamed. We should feel convicted of sin. We should be asking what the matter is with men and women that they behave in such a manner. The very facts and circumstances should convict us of sin. But they do not! And they do not because we always say that it is somebody else, never ourselves. It never comes home to us. But the Bible does bring it home to us. It addresses us and puts the plain unvarnished truth about ourselves to us directly and individually. And we need that.

The *second* reason why people do not believe the Christian message is that they are ignorant about the true nature of the Christian faith, and this, of course, is the tragedy of tragedies. They think they know what the Christian faith is, but they do not; they have a fundamental misconception and misunderstanding with regard to it.

So, in the light of these two fundamental and initial errors and fallacies, the Bible keeps on putting the two things together before us. That is why it is such a wonderful book. There is no end to the ways in which it does it: that is the proof that it is God's book. It gives it as direct teaching, and then it says, 'If you can't take it like that, take it in a picture or an illustration; take it in a bit of history'—that is why it gives us all this history. It says, 'Look at that man, look how he started, look how he ended. If you will not believe the teaching, look at this man's life. There is the truth for you, in a picture, in a bit of human history.' And then it takes up these comparisons, these illustrations.

Now all these are simply given to us in the great goodness and compassion of God, in an endeavour to bring the truth home to us simply and directly; and that is what we have in this first psalm which was undoubtedly written by David, who was moved by the Holy Spirit to do so. David was anxious to give this message to his contemporaries and he seems to be saying, 'Listen, there are two types of people in this world, and only two: the godly and the ungodly. And happiness depends upon whether you are one or the other. So how can I bring this truth home to the people?' Then he tells us, in general in the first two verses, some of the obvious characteristics of these two men—the godly and the ungodly. 'Yes,' says David, 'but even that is not enough; people are blind, they cannot see this, they cannot see the truth about themselves; they cannot see the truth about godliness. How can I put it to them?'

Tree or chaff?

So he goes on, and here he uses an illustration in order to try to help us to see the essence of this matter, the truth about ourselves, the truth about the godly or the Christian man or woman. And this is the picture that he uses: he says that the difference between the godly and the ungodly is the difference between a *tree* and *chaff*. He pictures a tree by the side of a river, and then there is a heap of chaff. 'So then,' he says in effect, 'if you can't see it in terms of direct teaching—when I talk about 'the counsel of the ungodly' and 'the way of sinners' and 'the seat of the scornful'—then try to see it like this.' So if you are concerned about this whole problem of life and of living, of happiness and of peace and joy, then the first, indeed the only, question I must ask is this: What are *you* like? What is your life like? Are you like a tree or are you like a heap of chaff? It must be one or the other.

The godly man is 'like a tree planted by the rivers of water, that bringeth forth his fruit in his season; his leaf also shall not wither; and whatsoever he doeth shall prosper. The ungodly are not so . . .' They are not like that. So what are they like? 'Oh,' he says, 'they are like the chaff which the wind driveth away.'

Now this is a tremendous thing. We are only in this world once; what is more important than that every one of us should know at this moment what kind of a person we are? I do not care how long you have lived. What is your life like? Does it resemble a tree or a heap of chaff?

So let us work this out together. In the last analysis, I do not care what will happen in the coming year. 'But', says somebody, 'that's callous!' No, what I mean is this: I do not care in the matter of my own condition and my own fundamental happiness. If my happiness is contingent upon things that may or may not take place, then I do not have any happiness and I will never have it. Happiness, blessedness, is that which renders us immune to the changing scenes of time and the vicissitudes and the circumstances and accidents of life.

So there is nothing more important than this. Let us examine it, therefore, and the first thing I find is that the whole trouble is that people do not know the truth about themselves or the truth about Christianity. They do not realise that the difference between the two is profound and radical. They tend to think that the difference between being a Christian and not being a Christian is only one of degree; for all people are really one, and they are all really alike except that there are certain particular differences of degree. 'Christians', they say, 'are people who do not do certain things that other people do, and vice versa. But there is no essential difference.'

The world always objects to the notion that there is an essential difference between the Christian and the non-Christian. So they tend to think that people make themselves Christians by making New Year resolutions, by deciding to drink less or to do something else less, and to improve themselves a bit and try to do a little more good. But they make themselves Christians. It is only a question of a slight change or adaptation; it is like a modification, an improvement on what they once were.

Or they may go further and think that Christians are people who have added something to their lives which they did not have before, and which those who are not Christians still do not have. But essentially they are still the same. I have sometimes put it like this: I get the impression that many people think that the only difference between the Christian and the non-Christian is like that between two books. The main body of the book is the same in both cases, so what is the difference? Ah, one of them has an appendix, and in the appendix it says that this man is a Christian. He is exactly the same as the other man in every other respect. If you meet him from Monday to Saturday, there is no difference. But on Sunday, this man goes to church, the other man does not. That is in the appendix: something he adds on. Otherwise there is nothing in it really, except that he tries to live a better life and so on.

That is the common notion with regard to this whole matter; that the difference between the Christian and the non-Christian is a very slight one, and is simply a difference in certain respects. But this picture in the psalm gives the lie direct to that once and for ever.

We do not have a comparison here between two trees. It is not the difference between an oak tree and a larch, or between some majestic pine and a blackthorn or something like that. No! he is not comparing trees. He is comparing a tree with a heap of chaff. And the Psalmist does that, of course, in order to bring this point perfectly clearly before our minds, that the difference is as deep and as radical and as essential as a difference can possibly be. We say it is 'the difference between chalk and cheese' but this difference is even bigger than that.

The fact is, says the Psalmist, that there is nothing common at all between the two. It is a complete contrast. I wonder whether we have all realised that? Have we realised that the difference between the Christian and the non-Christian is not a matter of conduct or of behaviour? It is the difference of nature. Now that is all-important, because many an ungodly man or woman can live quite a good life, judged morally and ethically. There are many very good people in the world, good from the standpoint of morals and of social customs and habits, and so on. There are many people like that who are very good in that sense, yet who are not Christians at all.

'Why do you say that they are not Christians?' asks someone. My main reason is that they have not got the same nature as the Christian. The Bible is full of this sort of thing. If you judge a man by the usual canons of judgment applied by people to one another, you would undoubtedly come to the conclusion that Esau was a much nicer and much better man than Jacob; he seems, as we put it, to have been a 'more decent fellow'; he seems to have had better characteristics in his personality. And yet the Bible says that the man who was loved by God was Jacob. Why? Because God does not judge by the outward appearance. God judges by the heart. God is interested in what a man is, not simply in what he does.

> The rank is but the guinea's stamp,
> The man's the gowd for a' that,

says Robert Burns, and I would apply his message in this much higher and spiritual sense. It is not the appearance, it is not the veneer that a man can put on; it is what he is, what his nature is, what he is in the depths and the vitals of his being.

That is what is brought out so wonderfully by the comparison here in the psalm. Are you a tree or are you like a heap of chaff, a collection of particles—nondescript, as I shall show you?

Now, that I may prove my contention, turn to the New Testament and you find that in showing the difference between the Christian and the non-Christian, the New Testament puts it in terms like these. It says that a Christian is someone who is 'born again'. Now there is the same radical point. 'Before you can become a Christian,' said our Lord to Nicodemus, 'you need to be born again.' Nicodemus patently thought that it was a question of adding on to what he had got. He went to our Lord seeking an interview, and he said, 'Master, I have been watching you and listening to you. You are much further advanced than I am, though I am a Master of Israel; what is this extra?' 'It is not a question of extras', says our Lord. 'Verily, verily, I say unto thee, except a man be born again, he cannot see the kingdom of God' (John 3:1-5). It is a rebirth that is necessary. These are the New Testament terms. A *regeneration*: we must be generated anew. There was nothing there; there has to be an act of generation. There is to be a kind of conception leading to a birth; nothing less than that.

Look at its other terms. It talks about a *new creation*: 'Therefore if any man be in Christ,' says the apostle Paul, 'he is a new creature' (2 Cor. 5:17). He is not just a little bit better than he was; he is not slightly different from the man who is not a Christian; he is a new creature, a new creation. The God who created at the beginning has created something new here that was not there before.

That is how the New Testament puts it. David puts it in a familiar illustration, but he has really got the whole truth, has he not? You have it explicitly in the teaching of the New Testament, but it is exactly the same.

Take one other further illustration in the New Testament: it is the difference, says Paul to the Ephesians, between death and *life*. 'And you hath he quickened, who were dead in trespasses and sins' (Eph. 2:1). Dead! Death: life! That is the contrast. And here it is before us in Psalm 1 in terms of a contrast between a tree growing by the side of a river and just a heap of chaff.

The details of the difference

So, having established that this is a very profound difference, I want to take you through the details of the difference.

I am doing this because I want you to be a happy man or woman. I want you to be a blessed person, and, thank God, I have a message that can make you that. I am not doing it: I am simply a mouthpiece. I want to show you what David puts before us here in this wonderful illustration, as the Spirit of God will enable me to do so. If your life is nothing but chaff, you will never be happy. Indeed, you will be eternally miserable if you go out of this world like that. Nothing is more important than that you should see the truth about yourself. Listen, therefore, to the difference as it is worked out by this comparison.

Nothing but a husk

The ungodly is like a heap of chaff. The other man is like a tree. What, therefore, is the difference? First, the ungodly is nothing but a relic, a remnant. He is nothing but a ruin and a wreck. What is chaff? Chaff is that which remains when you have taken the grain out. The grain is the kernel, and round it is this covering, this husk; and then in the process of winnowing or threshing you take out the grain with its food and its life, its value and its power, and what is left—the refuse—is the chaff.

So what David is telling us about this man who is ungodly, who is not a Christian, is that he is nothing but a husk; he is nothing but the covering, that which is left when everything that is vital and of value has gone. This is a very wonderful picture. The Bible, when you turn to its great doctrinal statements, puts it all like this. It says, 'What is the truth about man in sin and why is it that people are not blessed? Why is it that they are not happy? Well,' says the Bible, 'the answer is that man has fallen. He is a lost soul. He has lost his soul. He has lost his life. He is dead in trespasses and sins. He is nothing but a husk, the kernel has gone. He is nothing but the integument, the outer covering; all the value of the thing itself has gone.'

Now what this all means is that men and women, as they are by nature and as they are born into this world, are not real men and women at all. The greatest thing, the noblest thing about them, as God originally created them, has gone. Do you think God made men and women as they are to be seen in this world at this moment? Is that God's creation? Look at that poor helpless drunkard; look at that poor person who has fallen into some other sin; look at the miser; look at the ambitious person. Did God create such things? Of course he did not! God never created men and women like that. That is the husk, the refuse, the chaff. The vital thing is not there, it has gone, been lost; the soul is lost. That is why the Son of God, when he was in this world, said, 'For the Son of man is come to seek and to save that which was lost' (Luke 19:10).

The precious grain. What is this? Well, when God made man and woman he made them in his own image, and it is the image which has been lost. Men and women were made by God and for God; they were made in the image and likeness of God. That was their relationship to God. They were made as the companions of God; they were like God. They were made upright; they were given an original righteousness like that of God himself. They enjoyed God and companionship and fellowship with him. They had a spiritual faculty. They were never happier than when they were in that spiritual realm having communion with God. The word of God and the things of God—they were their great delight.

But they have fallen. They are not like that now. That is exactly what has gone. The original goodness, where is it? The enjoyment of God, where is it? The spiritual faculty, where is it? I ask you directly, is it in you or have you lost it?

39

Is there nothing left but chaff, the outer covering, the mere integument?

What David is saying here is the message of the whole Bible. As you look at men and women as they are in sin, as the result of the Fall, what you are seeing is nothing but the covering, nothing but the body and a kind of body of psychical life. That is the life men and women are living today; it is not a spiritual life, it is a psychical life.

It is not surprising that some scientists say that man is nothing but an animal. You look at man, as he is in sin, and you see nothing but an animal that lives to eat, and to drink, and to indulge in sex. I really do not see much difference! The way people are living is very reminiscent of the farm-yard. Indeed, it is reminiscent, sometimes, even of the jungle.

But that is the refuse, the chaff. That is not man: the great thing that came from God has been lost, it has gone. There is nothing left but ruins. As a hymn-writer has prayed, 'The ruins of my soul repair'.

An old Puritan living three hundred years ago once said that man, as a result of the Fall and of sin, is like many an old castle or a great old house that you can see sometimes in the country. You go along a road and you see a ruin which is all grown over with ivy and moss, an obvious ruin. So you go to examine it, and there you find a tablet, which says, 'So-and-so once lived here.' It was once the ancestral home of some great nobleman. It is nothing now but a mass of ruins with children playing in it, and the walls fallen down, and all the nettles and the thorns. Yet the tablet says, 'So-and-so once lived here.' And, said the Puritan, that is man. He is nothing but a ruin on which there is a notice which says, 'God once lived here.'

The image of God was once here. This was a noble creature, as that was once a noble building. But you are not seeing the real thing: you are seeing the ruins. Here is man as the result of sin and of the Fall. He is nothing but a remnant. Chaff! Without the wheat, without the kernel, without the germ, without the life. God once lived here.

So I want anybody who is not a Christian to see themselves as they are. You will not believe in Christ until you see your need of him. You will not believe in Christ until you see the ruin that you are. You will not turn to Christ and believe the gospel until you see that you are nothing but chaff— refuse, a relic, a ruin. But the Christian is a tree, and a tree is an organism, is it not? It is not a mere remnant. There is a wholeness about a tree. And that is the essential difference between the godly and the ungodly.

No form

But the second thing about chaff is that it has no form at all. It is just a heap of dust, the scrapings, the shavings, as it were, of the husk. And there it is in a pile, in a heap. It looks like this now, but it will not look like that in five minutes. The wind will move it a little. There it is, a shapeless mass.

And that is the ungodly, says the Psalmist. The truth about men and women in sin is that they have lost their character. It is difficult to define them. There is no pattern to their lives; they are always changing. You never know what they believe; you never know what they will do. Why? Because there is no form to their lives. There is no governing principle, and that is why it is so difficult to define such people.

The Bible says that we are all either godly or ungodly. But then look at the ungodly. From the great philosopher to the man who does not think at all; from the highly respected person to the profligate sinner, all are ungodly. What a shapeless mass it is; there is no rhyme nor reason. You cannot really define it, but there it is, just a conglomeration of scrapings. There is no form, no beauty, no symmetry.

But look at the tree for a moment. What a difference! This is the godly man. He is like a tree, and the whole point about a tree is that it has form, the trunk and the branches. Have you noticed the symmetry? There is nothing more beautiful than a tree—I am one of those people who thinks that a tree is much more beautiful than a flower. It does not matter; we all have our own opinion about that—but, oh, examine a tree and look at the balance, the consistency, as it were, that is so characteristic of it.

Now this is the truth about the godly man. He is not something indefinable. Christians are not people who have some vague nice feeling about themselves and who feel now and again like doing a bit of good. That is not Christianity! Christianity is not a shapeless collection of nice feelings and sentiments. It is definable, easily recognisable. It is like a tree. There is a balance about the life of Christian men and women. They have a doctrine and a practice. They have an understanding and an emotion. This is the great characteristic of these people who are godly, who are in Christ, and who belong to the realm of the spiritual and of the unseen.

Is there form in your life? Is there a shape to it? Is there consistency? Is there balance? Is there beauty? Ask yourself some simple questions. What is my life? Can I tell? Can I give an account of it, or can I not? It is one or the other.

No roots

The third point is this: another very striking difference between a tree and a heap of chaff is that the tree has roots, the heap of chaff has not. There it is: somebody has brushed it together, it is lying on the surface, it is not attached, everything is moving. Breathe on it and you will make it move. If the wind comes, says the Psalmist, it is gone.

'Chaff which the wind driveth away.' It does not drive away a tree because it has roots. Here is a tremendously important point: the tragedy about the man who is not godly, who is not a Christian, is that he is rootless. Or, if you prefer it, he has no foundations. It is a superficial life, it is all on the surface. Of course, it can be made to look attractive; an artist can do something even with a heap of chaff. But it is still all on the surface, all without weight. There are no really fixed principles there; there is nothing established.

What do you really know about life? What do you know about death? How do you meet the possible things that may happen in the future? These are the questions. And the truth about the godless man and woman is that they have no roots. They are utterly insecure; they do not know what will happen, and when it does happen, they do not know what to do about it. A 'wind of change' can move them. They are subject to it all; it is all contingent.

Oh, there are thousands of men and women like that in our great cities. There is many a poor wife tonight expecting her husband home and all she can say is, 'If he doesn't meet so-and-so he will be home at this time; if he does, then I don't know when I may see him.' He is rootless; he is all on the surface; it depends whether the wind blows, whom he may meet, what is going to happen to him. And these things determine his life. Ah, this godless life is insecure, it is a life that is always changing. You find these people change their views, they change their cults and they change their religions. As we are told of the people Paul found at Athens, the Stoics and the Epicureans, the most sophisticated people of the first century, they 'spent their time in nothing else, but either to tell, or to hear some new thing' (Acts 17:21). And the clever people who are godless are still doing that. 'Have you heard this?' they say. 'Have you heard the latest?' There are some new cults, some new treatment, some new idea, and after them they go. Then if that does not work, they will try the other. They are always spending their time in hearing or telling of some new thing. Like the chaff they are rootless, with no foundation to their lives.

But the Christian, the godly man or woman, is altogether different. Their 'delight is in the law of the Lord' and they meditate in it day and night. We are told about them in the New Testament that they are 'rooted and built up in him, and stablished in the faith' (Col. 2:7). And this is something that needs to be emphasised at this present time. Christians are not just nice people, not just good ones; they are not just people who have pleasant and happy feelings. No, Christians are men and women who know what they believe and they know *whom* they believe.

I grieve to have to say this, but I do not care who says it, on a television interview or anywhere else: the man who says that a Christian is just someone who recognises the ethical teaching of Christ and then does his best to follow it, is a man who knows nothing about Christianity. No, Christians believe a body of doctrine. They are like a tree which has roots; it is held by something; it is fixed to something; the tendrils are grasping something. That is why it is not carried away by the wind. And the body of doctrine does not stop at believing in God. Of course, some say that you do not even need to believe that. You can look forward to meeting atheists in heaven. What have we come to? It is chaff to say that a man can believe or disbelieve anything he likes in this world and still go to heaven. That is to say, in effect, that the chaff becomes a tree; that there is no difference. That is a lie! It is not true. The tree has its roots and the roots are fixed.

What is this faith? It is faith in the Son of God, the faith that says that Jesus of Nazareth is the only begotten Son of God. It says that he was born of a virgin; it was a miraculous birth; he had no human father; it was a unique act of God. The Holy Spirit came upon Mary and he was 'conceived of the Holy Ghost'. It says that he proved that by his miracles and by his teaching. It says that he went to the cross on Calvary deliberately, because it was the only way whereby he could save us. That he took our sins upon himself and bore their punishment, and that our guilt was laid on him. God smote that guilt in him, punished him for us, and thereby gave us free forgiveness. Faith believes that men and women become Christians not as a result of a good life or good deeds, but because they believe that Christ died for them and rose again, and that God has put Christ's righteousness upon them.

That is what Christians believe. They believe in the resurrection. Of course they do!—the literal, physical, bodily resurrection. They believe in the person of the Holy Spirit and that he was sent upon the Church on the Day of Pentecost. These are the things to which the roots of the Christian man and woman cling; they are entwined about them, and hold on to them, and out of them everything else comes. There are roots in the Christian; there is nothing in the chaff. The chaff does not know what it believes. It does not know where it is, and that it is why it is always changing, and that is why it is always insecure. The Christian, you see, is entirely different. 'Be ready', says the apostle Peter, 'always to give an answer to every man that asketh you a reason of the hope that is in you' (1 Pet. 3:15).

Come, my friends, we are living in a dying world. I cannot afford to take risks; I will have to give an account of my stewardship of my preaching. I may be asked about your soul, did I make it plain and clear to you? What I am asking you, therefore, is this: you say you are like a tree and that you do

45

not belong to the chaff. Well then, I ask you, do you believe the things I have been putting before you? Do you believe that unless you believe those things, you are not a Christian? However good you may be, however moral, however much good you may do, however wonderful your philosophy may be, if you do not believe the bare essentials, the irreducible minimum of this Christian faith, you are chaff and nothing but chaff. The godless have no roots; it is the tree that has roots.

No life

Then another thing I would ask you to consider and to work out for yourselves is this: the difference between a heap of chaff and a tree is the difference between lifelessness and life. There is no life in a heap of chaff, and you will never get growth out of it. If you leave it there on the ground for a thousand years, it will never add to itself. Why? Because it has no life in it. But a tree! Why, the whole point about a tree is that it has life in it and it can grow; but not so that chaff, which is the same at the end as it was at the beginning. Well, that is not quite true—it is worse! A lot of dirt and mud has got attached to it and bits of it have blown about. All sorts of things are added to it, but there is never any improvement, never anything better.

Now that is what the Bible says about people in sin. It does not matter what they do, they do not improve themselves or add to themselves; they do not grow; they do not develop. 'But what', you may say, 'about science or music or art?' I tell you that if men and women do not know this truth of God as it is in Christ Jesus, they will end where they began. No! they will be worse than when they began.

The wise man, Solomon, in writing Ecclesiastes, said 'Vanity of vanities, all is vanity' (Eccles. 1:2). But the poets have said it also. The greatest English poets have looked back with nostalgia across their lives: 'O,' they say, 'that I were still the man I once was!' Wordsworth writes,

> Our birth is but a sleep and a forgetting;
> The Soul that rises with us, our life's Star,
>   Hath had elsewhere its setting,
>   And cometh from afar;
>   Not in entire forgetfulness,
>   And not in utter nakedness,
> But trailing clouds of glory do we come
>   From God, who is our home:
> Heaven lies about us in our infancy!
> Shades of the prison-house begin to close
>   Upon the growing Boy,
> But he beholds the light, and whence it flows,
>   He sees it in his joy;
> The Youth, who daily farther from the east
>   Must travel, still is Nature's priest,
>   And by the vision splendid
>   Is on his way attended;
> At length the Man perceives it die away,
> And fade into the light of common day.

Where is the dream? Where is the ecstasy? 'Change and decay in all around I see', says Henry Francis Lyte. And so these great poets, writing about life, support the teaching of the Bible.

And your vast knowledge and learning—where does it bring you? Does it really help you to live? Does it really help you to be strong? Does it really help you to die? Does it throw any light upon eternity? Look at the great men dying; watch them even as they are decaying before they die. They are objects of misery and compassion, and we feel like saying, 'It's a pity he doesn't go before he'll be too sad even to look at.' Chaff!

But you never speak like that about a tree, do you? Oh no, the whole thing is different. A tree has life in it. Turn to the New Testament and you read about people starting out as babes in Christ. Here is something different. You see, the difference between a babe and a heap of chaff is that whereas the chaff can never grow and develop, a baby, though he cannot speak or reason, has got life in him. He can grow and develop, and he does so. John writes, in his first Epistle, to the children, to the young men and to the old men. There is a difference, a development. There is a growth always possible in a tree, and to me that is one of the most glorious things about this Christian life. The more I go on in it, the more I am thrilled in it.

Oh, the vastness of the knowledge, as one brings one's little mind to these mighty epistles of the apostle Paul, and sees him handling what Thomas Carlyle called 'the immensities and the infinities'—this truth of God. 'That ye . . . may be able to comprehend', he says, 'with all saints what is the breadth, and length, and depth, and height; and to know the love of Christ, which passeth knowledge' (Eph. 3:18-19). What is this? It is a never-ebbing sea, and one goes on out, ever forward into the depths, the deep things of God. One grows in knowledge, and one grows in grace, and there is infinite, eternal possibility of development and of advance. Oh, the difference between the godly life and the ungodly life! The difference between the tree and the chaff! The difference between life and death—something inert, inanimate and lifeless, and that which is full of life.

No fruit

The last thing which I must refer to is the fruit. There is never any fruit coming from chaff. Chaff is always useless, and the ungodly life is a life of chaff. It never gives anyone real satisfaction. The apostle Paul reminds the Romans that they were once sinners and slaves of sin, and he puts this tremendous question to them that I would put to everyone: 'For when ye were the servants of sin, ye were free from righteousness'; you did not have any. Then comes the question: 'What fruit had ye then in those things whereof ye are now ashamed? for the end of those things is death' (Rom. 6:20-21). 'Listen,' says Paul in effect, 'Tell me, what real fruit did you have in those things when you were doing them? Did they give you real satisfaction? Did they give you real joy? Did they give you true and clean happiness? Did they give you anything? I know', he says, 'you are ashamed of them now, but did they even give you any real satisfaction *then*? And therein is death.' How true that is! The life of sin never gives any satisfaction. You think for a moment that it will; you think you have it, then you have lost it. There is nothing to feed upon, nothing left, nothing to ruminate upon. There is no real value. What does lust really give you? What does greed or ambition really give you? They are never satisfied. The ambitious man is never satisfied. He always wants more, and he is always afraid that somebody else is coming up behind him and that he will be robbed of his position. Never peace; never joy; never any real happiness. It is chaff.

'I lay in dust life's glory dead', said George Matheson. He had come to see the truth about himself, that it was a life of chaff. And so, I ask you this final question: What is the nature, the character of your life? Is it chaff or is it like a tree? This is what the Bible tells us: 'All flesh is as grass, and all the glory of man as the flower of grass.' The wind of the Lord blows upon it and, as a result, 'the grass withereth, and the flower thereof falleth away' (1 Pet. 1:24). That is it! All the glory of man.

> The boast of heraldry, the pomp of pow'r,
>   And all that beauty, all that wealth e'er gave,

Awaits alike th' inevitable hour.
The paths of glory lead but to the grave.

Thomas Gray

And many a man who has lived through this world and thought he has achieved a great deal, finds at the end that he is nothing but a heap of chaff.

Think of the people living today who have been feeding on the filth of the law-courts' reports in their Sunday newspapers, who are living to drink and to gamble and to indulge in other things. What have they got? What life? What do they have at the end? It is nothing but refuse, chaff. That is the life of the ungodly. The glittering prizes of this world are nothing but chaff. They have nothing to give the soul, nothing to give the spirit, nothing to give real joy and lasting peace or a solid treasure. Men and women are chasing bubbles, and the moment they touch them they have exploded in their hands and there is nothing there. They have nothing but a heap of refuse; the kernel, the life, the grain has gone; there is nothing but the remnants, the ruins.

That is a man or a woman without God, as they are left to themselves. But the Son of God came, as I have reminded you, 'to seek and to save that which is lost'. So if you find that there is nothing but refuse and chaff left in your life; if there is nothing of the man or woman that God originally made— then cry out to God, confess it to him; acknowledge it and do not try to defend yourself. Say, 'I am nothing; create me anew.' And he will do it. He sent his Son into this world to save the refuse, the ruins of the soul, and he has power sufficient to do it. He has borne the punishment and the guilt of our sin, for being chaff when we were meant to be trees. He has died for you. And you will know the life-giving and new-creating power of God through the blessed Holy Spirit.

3
The tree

And he shall be like a tree planted by
the rivers of water, that bringeth forth his
fruit in his season; his leaf also shall not
wither; and whatsoever he doeth shall prosper.
The ungodly are not so: but are like the chaff
which the wind driveth away.
(Psalm 1:3-4)

In the last sermon we were looking at the Psalmist's picture of the ungodly—the chaff. But now, let us turn to the positive side. Christians, he says, are altogether different from that, and we saw some of the differences when we considered the form of the tree, its roots, its comeliness, the fact that it has life, that it can grow and develop, that it can bear fruit. But I want to go beyond that now and work out what the Psalmist says in detail here.

The man who is godly, he says—who is in the right relationship to God, who is a Christian, who is truly blessed—is a man who is 'like a tree planted by the rivers of water'. What a contrast! And the question that comes to us must be this: How does one become like this tree? 'I see the comparison,' says someone; 'I can see the point you're establishing that there really is nothing in common between these two, but that it is altogether different to be a Christian. How, then, can one become a Christian? I see the uselessness of the other life. I see its emptiness and its vanity. I see that it's of no value, finally, to the man himself or to anybody else. So I should like to know how one becomes like this tree.' Now remember, it is only a picture, an illustration, but it is a very vivid one and it does lead us to some of the most important answers to that very question. Therefore, let us look at them together.

Planted

This is the answer as it seems to be displayed here. It is, *firstly*, that we become Christians, godly persons, as the result of something that is done to us, something that happens to us. 'He shall be like a tree *planted* . . .' It is put there, and it is put there by somebody. 'It is planted by the rivers of water', says the Psalmist; so it is not a natural growth appearing at that given place—that is surely implicit in this word 'planted'. Someone has come along, made a place for it, put it in—planted it there. It is the Psalmist's term, and he uses it because the whole of the Bible uses it. This is of the very essence of the biblical message. This is how one becomes a Christian and a godly person. In other words, no one is born a Christian into this world. It does not matter where you are born. I trust that nobody still believes the nonsense about 'Christian' countries, and that we are Christians because we are born in one of them, or into a particular family that happens to be Christian. There is no such thing! No one is a Christian by nature; we are all, according to the Bible, the 'children of wrath' (Eph. 2:3) by nature—every one of us. 'There is none righteous, no, not one' (Rom. 3:10). We are all born in sin, 'shapen in iniquity' (Ps. 51:15). So it is not something natural.

Or you may like to consider it this way. This tree does not just grow up there; and, in exactly the same way, no one grows up gradually to be a Christian; that is impossible. It does not matter what the circumstances are or what the surroundings, no one just grows up to be a Christian. It does not just happen as it happened in the case of Topsy—'just growed'! That is never true of any Christian. Nor are we Christians as a result of anything that we do ourselves, to ourselves, or for ourselves. A tree cannot plant itself. That is the very essence of the picture that the Psalmist has chosen. It has to be planted by somebody else. And that is precisely what happens to everybody who is a Christian; everybody who becomes a godly person.

Now, I want to make this plain and clear, because there is such confusion at this point. There are so many who think that some of us are born Christians. We were always taken to Sunday school or church, always believed in God, always said our prayers, have always been Christians. But there is no such thing! It is impossible. That does not mean to say that you may not have become a Christian at a very early age, and that you may not be able to put your finger on the particular point when you became one. All I am saying is that nobody is born as a Christian or is one by nature.

And nothing that any one of us does ever makes us a Christian. It does not matter how good a life you live. Now, is this clear? We must be certain of our foundations. Is there anyone who still thinks that you make yourself a Christian by doing anything at all? I do not care what it is. You do not make yourself a Christian even by praying or by reading the Bible. You do not make yourself a Christian by doing good, even by giving all your goods to feed the poor—read 1 Corinthians 13. Do what you like; do everything; and you are still not a Christian.

> Not the labours of my hands
> Can fulfil Thy law's demands;

Could my zeal no respite know,
Could my tears for ever flow,
All for sin could not atone . . .
Augustus Toplady

No, no! The tree is planted, and this is the message; it is planted by another and not by itself. Which leads us, of course, to the very heart of the gospel. What makes anybody a Christian is what God has done in and through his only begotten beloved Son, our Lord and Saviour Jesus Christ, and by the application of all that to individual persons by the Holy Spirit. Planted! It is the action of another, something that is done to us, that happens to us. This is the gospel. 'For God so loved the world, that he gave [sent] his only begotten Son, that whosoever believeth in him should not perish, but have everlasting life' (John 3:16). There it is! That whosoever believeth in him should not remain as chaff but might become a tree planted by the rivers of water. It is just another way of saying that. But, you notice, the action is *God's*. The Bible is a book which records the activity of God, not man. This is not a record of man seeking and searching after God and striving to find him; it is the exact opposite. It is man going astray and God coming after him. As he came down into the Garden of Eden at the very beginning when man had sinned, so he has been coming down ever since, and he came down supremely in the person of his only begotten Son, our Lord and Saviour, Jesus Christ.

This planting, you see, just means this. It is what God was doing when he brought about the incarnation; when he sent his Son from the eternal and everlasting glory and caused him to be born out of the virgin's womb. That is what makes us Christians. It is not good, moral, ethical teaching which we strive after. What makes us Christians is that God sent his

54

Son into this world. God has 'visited and redeemed his people' (Luke 1:68). It is the incarnation, and all that followed.

What makes us Christians is not only the birth of Jesus, the Son of God; it is his only perfect life, rendering perfect obedience to the law of God. It is his sacrificial, atoning death upon the cross on Calvary's hill: this is the planting. This is God's action. This is what makes us Christians. That is why he came. He would never have come, he would never have died on the cross, if we could have been made Christians, godly men and women, in any other way or manner. It is God's action that matters. 'The Lord hath laid on him the iniquity of us all' (Isa. 53:6). 'For he hath made him to be sin for us, who knew no sin; that we might be made the righteousness of God in him' (2 Cor. 5:21). God laid our sins on his Son and smote him and struck him. It involves all this; this tremendous activity on the part of this great planter who plants the tree. It is his action, his activity. And then, as the result of God smiting him with the sword of his wrath on the cross, the Son died and his body was taken down and buried in a grave. Then, by the mighty power of God, he was raised again from the dead. Death and hell were conquered. He burst asunder the bonds of death. He was raised even unto heaven itself, and there he is, seated at the right hand of God and, being seated there, he sent down the blessed Holy Spirit on the day of Pentecost to produce the results of all this activity in men and women as they believe in him.

So when Peter preached on the day of Pentecost, and the people began to cry out saying, 'Men and brethren, what shall we do?', his answer was: 'Repent, and be baptised every one of you in the name of Jesus Christ'. And then, he said, 'ye shall receive the gift of the Holy Ghost' (Acts 2:38). It is God, and God alone, therefore, who makes anybody a Christian. 'Like a tree planted . . .'

Have we really understood this, or are we still imagining that Christianity is something that we can produce? There are very many texts which show that this is not so. 'For we are his workmanship,' says the apostle Paul, 'created in Christ Jesus unto good works . . .' (Eph. 2:10). 'But as many as received him, to them gave he power to become the children of God, even to them that believe on his name: which were born, not of blood, nor of the will of the flesh, nor of the will of man, but of God' (John 1:12-13). And it is the same everywhere in the Bible. So that Christian men and women must say with the apostle Paul, 'But by the grace of God I am what I am' (1 Cor. 15:10). They have nothing to boast about because they have done nothing; it has been done to them; it is this operation of the almighty God upon them and their souls.

Created

The *second* principle is this: What, then, is it that happens to them? 'What do you mean by *planting*?' asks someone. 'This is only a picture. What is the spiritual content, the spiritual truth?' Well, what it means is this: somebody has to create this tree, and, having created it, he has to take it and to put it into this position 'by the rivers of water'. Let me unfold this wonderful picture to you and put it in more direct New Testament terms. This is the operation of the Holy Spirit. Before people can become Christians, obviously, from this definition, they need new life; they need a new nature. You do not become a Christian by deciding to imitate Christ or to follow him, or by trying to put the Sermon on the Mount into practice. You try that, and you will find you cannot do it. That is the experience of the greatest saints the world has ever known.

Nor, as we have seen, is it a matter of any addition to what we are or of improving what we have; it is not that at all.

What makes us Christians is that God creates us anew. He puts new life into us. He puts a new principle into us. We become new creations, new men and women. Do you realise that? The Christian is, as I showed in the last sermon, absolutely and essentially different. This heap of refuse, this chaff, has no life in it: but the Christian is like a tree and somebody has put life into the tree. The Creator has put it there, and he does the same thing to everybody who becomes a Christian. 'Ye must be born again', says our Lord to Nicodemus (John 3:7). You need to have life put into you, you need to be regenerated before you can become a Christian. That is great New Testament doctrine, the essence of Christian doctrine. So how does it happen?

Well, this planting—this is the most fascinating and wonderful thing—is God dealing with us and our souls by the Holy Spirit. He has prepared the life in his Son. Humanity was so rotten that it could not be improved; you must have a new start. In the Old Testament, we are told that God gave his law to the people and said, 'If you can keep this it will save you', but they could not. Nobody kept it, everybody failed. So God said in effect, 'There is only one way to save, and that is, I must start a new humanity. The first Adam fell and his progeny has fallen after him. I must send a second Adam. I must send another man. It is no use creating another man: he would fall as the first man fell. The first man was perfect, so if another perfect man is created he again will fall and succumb to the attacks and the onslaughts of the devil. 'So,' God said, 'I am going to make a new type of humanity: I will send my own Son, and he will take human nature unto himself.' Here is the head of a new humanity, the Son of God. He has life in him for men and women, he is truly man, so I can receive life from him. But how does that come to me? Now you see the meaning of the incarnation and his perfect spotless life of obedience and his death on the cross, his burial and his resurrection and ascension. There it is, there is salvation in him. But the question is, How can I can get that life? That is what I need. And the answer is that there is a power that can take you and plant you into it, put you into it. 'Like a tree planted by the rivers of water.'

Have you ever tried to plant a tree? There is the earth and you must dig it. You will need a spade and perhaps a fork and you must loosen it. You must do all that before you put your tree in. Then, after the tree is in, you put the earth back and you stamp it and press it down. Then the tree is all right. But that is quite a process, is it not? It is quite hard work some-times. In the same way, it is not an easy process that we go through to become Christians, and here are some of the things that the Holy Spirit does to us as he plants us in Christ Jesus.

Do you know anything about the work of conviction, this process of getting that earth broken up and dug, with the spade and the fork put in, pressed down by the foot, lifted up and the earth broken? Do you know anything about it? You cannot be a Christian without conviction of sin. This process involves a great deal of disturbance; we may have gone on living for years persuading ourselves that every-thing was all right, and refusing to think. Untoward events and circumstances would take place and we would never allow them to have their full weight of benefit upon us; but suddenly we are disturbed, we are taken hold of, and some-thing, we say, makes us think. And it is the Holy Spirit who is doing it.

This process of breaking up the ground can happen in a church service. You suddenly become aware of the fact that God is dealing with you: you are no longer just a spectator or a listener. You are no longer just a critic, sitting there, notebook in hand, making notes about things you do not like and do not agree with. All that stops, and you are aware that something is being done to you—you are being broken up. You no longer are detached from this, you are involved in it and you are aware that God is dealing with you, disturbing you, rousing you, convicting you, making you face questions, making you feel uncomfortable and unhappy. You want to defend yourself, I know, but it is because of what is happening to you. This is conviction of sin. So do you know anything about it?

And then, of course, it goes on to a realisation of the truth. You are what you are because God has not been in your life, you do not know him, and you have not lived to his glory and to his praise. You have not spent your time delighting in his law and meditating in it day and night. You have dismissed the Bible: 'It is played out,' you say; 'I believe in modern philosophy and modern science.' God has meant nothing at all to you. But now, you come to the realisation that that is why you are what you are. That is why you fail in life. That is why you are unhappy. That is why you have to spend so much time and money in trying to find happiness. And you never succeed. It is all because of this wrong relationship to God. The truth comes home. The Spirit brings it home. He says, 'There you are, there is God, and you have not lived under God and for God, but you have sinned against him.' You realise it now and you stop defending yourself.

Then you begin to feel hopeless and you say, 'What can I do?' The devil suggests that you start living a new life; start reading your Bible; start going to church; start doing good; and, perhaps, you foolishly listen to him and you go on doing that, as Martin Luther did before his conversion. But the more you do this, of course, the more you find out about the holiness of God and the darkness of your own soul. And it makes you feel absolutely hopeless and helpless.

And then the Spirit reveals to you this wonderful message of salvation that is here in the Bible; all the preparation for it in the Old, and then the coming of the Son of God, with all that I reminded you of just now. Suddenly you see it all and its relevance to you. And he says to you, 'Believe on the Lord Jesus Christ and you will be saved. Accept that truth, believe it is true for you; believe that the Son of God came from heaven in order to make you a new man, a new woman, to give you new life. He has taken your sins upon himself; you can be forgiven.' You suddenly begin to get a glimmer of insight into it and then you are led on to repentance, to an acknowledgment that you do not deserve this. You see that God would be fully justified if he punished you eternally. You are sorry for your sin, you want to leave it, you tell God so, you cast yourself upon his mercy, and you tell him, 'I do not understand it, but I believe this message of repentance and faith in the Lord Jesus Christ.'

It is the Spirit who makes you do all that. That is all a part of the preparation of this ground: the digging and the breaking up, and the sifting, and the preparation of the soil, as it were. All this is essential. Then, he comes and he takes hold of this new life and he puts it into you. This is the rebirth. This is the life put in and the tree put into its position and the ground put back and levelled and all that I have been describing.

Now that is what is emphasised in particular here by the Psalmist, and the picture is a wonderful one. 'It's like a tree', he says, 'planted'—yes, but he does not stop at that. It is not just a planted tree; it all depends where you plant it. The secret of the godly man, he says, is that he is 'like a tree planted *by the rivers of wate*r'. Not planted in a wilderness or on top of a mountain; no, planted by a great, majestic river flowing through a beautiful valley with a rich loam, with wonderful land surrounding it everywhere. That is where it is planted, and this, of course, is about as perfect a picture as you could possibly find of what happens when a man or a woman is born again and regenerated.

Life in Christ

The location is the thing that matters. Where is the tree planted? 'By the rivers of water.' Where is a Christian planted? Into Christ Jesus. Do you realise this? What makes men and women Christians is not that they are better than they were and are trying to be better still, and that they are trying to follow Christ. No, no. What makes us Christians is that we are taken and grafted into Christ; that we begin to receive of the life of Christ. The New Testament is full of this term, 'in Christ'. It tells us that we were all born in Adam (Rom. 5:14-18; 1 Cor. 15:22), and it is because we are all born 'in Adam' that we end as chaff. Now, says the New Testament, what you need is to be 'in Christ' (1 Cor. 15:22), in this new humanity. You need this new life that is in him. He said, 'I am come that they might have life, and that they might have it more abundantly' (John 10:10).

Again, here, in the psalm, the illustration works itself out. The characteristic of the soil by the side of a great river is that there is depth there. It is not just a light, loose, rocky soil with just a little surface layer of earth. No, no. Always by the side of a river there is this depth, this mud, this nutriment, this solidity. That is why the man plants the tree there; he wants it to become a majestic tree. So he puts it by the side of the river in that rich loam, that wonderful soil.

But how inadequate is even the best illustration! Do you know what it is that makes us Christians? It is that the life of God comes into our souls. Nothing less! Here is the soil; planted into Christ, the Son of God, we become partakers of the divine nature, and you cannot estimate the depth; it is the riches of the Godhead himself. The apostle Paul tells the Ephesians that he was praying for them, that they might be 'filled with all the fulness of God' (Eph. 3:19). In Christ, the man, we receive of this new humanity, this perfect humanity that is in him; that is what makes us Christians. It is an entirely new start. It is like being born again. It is like a new life altogether. There is a new principle put into us, a new disposition; something that was not there before.

But notice also the rivers of water, because the point about this tree is that it is not only in very good soil, but its roots go down and they spread, and the tendrils break out, and some of them actually get into the bed of the river. And there it draws its moisture from the rivers of water, so that the roots of the tree are in this river-bed with all its glorious moisture. This is a picture which tells us that Christians are men and women who draw all their life, their nutriment, their sustenance and everything from the Lord Jesus Christ himself. Let him say it for himself so that you do not think that I am inventing these things that I am putting before you! Listen to him. 'I am that bread of life,' he says. 'Your fathers did eat manna in the wilderness, and are dead. This is the bread which cometh down from heaven, that a man may eat thereof, and not die. I am the living bread which came down from heaven: if any man eat of this bread, he shall live for ever: and the bread that I will give is my flesh, which I will give for the life of the world. The Jews therefore strove among themselves, saying, How can this man give us his flesh to eat? Then Jesus said unto them, Verily, verily, I say unto you, Except ye eat the flesh of the Son of man, and drink his blood, ye have no life in you. Whoso eateth my flesh, and drinketh my blood, hath eternal life; and I will raise him up at the last day. For my flesh is meat indeed, and my blood is drink indeed. He that eateth my flesh, and drinketh my blood, dwelleth in me, and I in him. As the living Father hath sent me, and I live by the Father: so he that eateth me, even he shall live by me' (John 6:48-57).

The life, the sustenance, the moisture, everything comes out of this blessed river of life which is none other than the Son of God himself, who became incarnate and died and rose again in order that we might have it. He is the head, says Paul, out of which all comes. The head of the body is Christ, and he controls the entire body of which we are but parts (Eph. 4:15-16). And do you notice the Psalmist's emphasis upon 'the rivers of water'? There is an endless supply. It is as endless as God himself. We receive of the very life of God. We are partakers of the divine nature (2 Pet.1:4), filled with all the fulness of God.

That is Christianity. Never think again of it in terms of being just nice and good and moral and decent and better than somebody else. That's Pharisaism. I do not tell you to be a good man or woman; I say you are so bad you must be made 'a new man' (Eph. 4:24). You must be born again. I say you can have life from God, and this is what makes you a Christian. Nothing less. Planted by the rivers of water, drawing the life of Christ himself; planted into him; put into him; engrafted into him. These are all the New Testament terms suggested by the Psalmist in his wonderful illustration in this first psalm.

Do you see the logic? Firstly, you become a Christian as the result of what happens to you, not as the result of what you do. Secondly, what happens to you is that you are 'planted', placed in Christ. I ask you in the name of God before I go any further: Have you been planted in Christ? Have you been through this process in some shape or form? Have you been aware of the digging and the breaking up and the preparation, and have you known the blessed hands taking hold of you and putting you in Christ so that you know you are a new man or a new woman? Or has your idea been that you are making yourself a Christian, or that you have always been one, that you were brought up to be one—which is it? But you cannot be a Christian without knowing that he, the Spirit of God, has taken you and has planted you, has engrafted you into Christ himself. And then you say, Christ is my life. 'I live; yet not I, but Christ liveth in me: and the life which I now live in the flesh I live by the faith of the Son of God, who loved me, and gave himself for me' (Gal. 2:20). Can you say that? If you cannot, I take leave to doubt whether you are a Christian. Unless you feel that you are what you are solely as the result of what God has done to you through the Spirit, you are not a Christian. You may be very good; you may be religious, you may be highly moral, but you cannot be a Christian. It is God alone who makes Christians. And that is how he makes them.

Result

The third point will, perhaps, help us to answer the question I have just been putting. What is the result of this work of God which happens to Christian men and women? What is the result to which the operation of the Holy Spirit upon them leads? It is all here, and thank God for it. We saw something of it in the last sermon and we shall see more of it now, though I only give you my headings—I am ashamed that I am almost apologising for the length of this sermon; may God forgive me! Do you feel that it is too long? Do you want it to finish? If you do, you know nothing about Christianity. What is there in life but this? We are in a dying world, my friends. Great men have to die like everybody else. You may have to die at any moment. Do not boast too much about the scientific advances and developments; you cannot always deal with a virus infection, can you? So I am talking to you about eternal life which God alone can give. So then, I make no apology for going on and giving you my headings about the *results* to which this wonderful action of God upon the soul leads.

Fruit

Here is the first thing: 'He is like a tree planted by the rivers of water', and here is the first result—he 'bringeth forth his fruit in his season'. This means that the first thing that happens when people become Christians is that they really begin to function in the way they were meant to do. What is the function of a tree? It is to bring forth fruit. And this tree brings forth its fruit. We saw that the trouble with the chaff is that human beings were never meant to be like that. It is no good, profitless, a relic, the germ has gone. But now men and women are restored; they are now doing and being what they were meant to be. When they become Christians that image of God, that was defaced and more or less destroyed when Adam fell, is restored to them. The apostle Paul tells the Ephesians, 'But ye have not so learned Christ; if so be that ye have heard him, and have been taught by him, as the truth is in Jesus: that ye put off concerning the former conversation the old man, which is corrupt according to the deceitful lusts; and be renewed in the spirit of your mind; and that ye put on the new man, which after God is created in righteousness and true holiness' (Eph. 4:20-24). That means that when men and women become Christians, they have been born again; they have been created anew by God in righteousness and true holiness. That is what they lost in the Fall, as we saw; now it is given back to them and they are no longer those ruins with the notice saying 'God once dwelt here'. The thorns and the briars have been removed, and the ivy has been plucked off. He has sent his architect and his workman and he is back in residence. The image of God is restored to them and therefore they become people who are conscious once more of the dignity of manhood. They know what it is truly to be human, and they are not mere animals that are in the world to eat and drink and indulge their passions and desires. No, no. They are friends of God; they enjoy fellowship and communion with God, and they know they are meant to live to the glory of God. They are separated from the animals; they realise anew that they are meant to be the lords of creation and essentially different from the animal. The psychologist's view of human nature is nothing but the chaff; the biblical view of men and women is that they are in the image of God, full of the righteousness and holiness of the truth, and back again into God's likeness.

In season

But, secondly, the godly man bears his fruit, says the Psalmist, *in his season*, and I rather like this. That is the characteristic of the tree, is it not, that you can more or less prophesy when the fruit will be there. There is a regularity about it because it is obeying the law of its being. The tree has been so made and constituted that it produces its fruit at a given point. You begin to see the buds and then the flowers and then the maturity. Then the fruit begins to form, and that grows and develops, and then you can go and pick your fruit. I am told by the experts that you can almost do it to the day, apart from some curious accident in the weather. And the godly man and woman bear their fruit in its season. That means that they are not godly by fits and starts, or when the spasm takes them, or because it happens to be the beginning of a new year, or because somebody dies in the family, or because they have had an illness. No, no. They show steadiness, reliability; a life governed by truth, and a life based upon principles. It is not a rootless life: it is a life that is rooted in Christ and is drawing its regular supply from that glorious river of water that is flowing by.

And then for the fruit itself: what is it? 'The fruit of the Spirit', says Paul, 'is love, joy, peace, longsuffering, gentleness, goodness, faith, meekness, temperance' (Gal. 5:22-23). These are the things that begin to appear in a man or a woman who becomes a Christian. Now there are many who say they are Christians, but people often say, 'I know So-and-so who is always selfish and self-centred and she says she's a Christian.' All right, she may say so, but the fact that a man or a woman says that he or she is a Christian, as I have shown you, does not prove that they are. Christians produce fruit, and they produce it in season; and the fruit of the Spirit is love, joy, peace, long-suffering, and so on. It is a necessity. You cannot have the life of God in your soul and still produce those works of the flesh—fornication, adultery, drunkenness, licentiousness, jealousy—all those belong to the chaff. But the fruit of the Spirit, oh how different! That is the fruit that the Christian bears.

Delight

And then, of course—and we have already seen a little of this—'his delight is in the law of the Lord'. This is a very good test. Do you enjoy reading your Bible? Do you 'meditate in it day and night'? Do you want to know more about it? These are some of the fruit. But there are more. There is help to others. That is fruit. Somebody comes along and is hungry, so he takes the fruit and eats it. And Christians are people who can help others. You should be 'ready always', says the apostle Peter, to give 'a reason for the hope that is in you' (1 Pet. 3:15). Can you help people when they are in trouble? Can you tell somebody else how to become a Christian? Can you tell them what the Christian faith is? If you can't tell them, you are not a Christian. If you are a Christian, you can.

And you not only help them in that way but also in actual deeds of kindness and mercy and compassion. It is a simple fact of history to say that the greatest benefactors this world has ever known have been Christian people. Where did schools first come from? From the Christian church. Where did hospitals come from? From the Christian church. The oldest hospital in London is St Bartholomew's Hospital, which was started by a monk called Rahere over eleven centuries ago. Where did the end of slavery come from? From William Wilberforce, a converted Christian—a man who could tell you that he was once not a Christian and that then he was planted in Christ. Where did the Factory Acts come from? From Lord Shaftesbury, again a converted Christian. All the best and the noblest institutions in this country have come originally from Christian people. What about the Trades Unions? There is a lot of talk about them today. Do you know that they came from Christian people? Even a man like Lecky (a nineteenth-century historian) is prepared to admit that it was the Methodists converted in the eighteenth century who first began to see themselves as human beings and not as pigs, and who began to demand their rights. All these things have come in the wake of Christianity, as this tree bears fruit always in its season.

Prepared for everything

But not only shall the Christian bear his fruit in his season; thank God for this next thing too: 'his leaf also shall not wither'. I have already shown you that you must not think that your happiness is dependent on circumstances and events; because if it does, you may soon lose it. Who knows what is going to happen in the future? Are you afraid of it? Are you afraid of evil tidings? Do you say, 'Don't tell me', because you are afraid to hear them? Because if you are, I doubt whether you are a godly person. Indeed, I am sure you are not, because what I am told about the godly person is this—it is in another psalm—'Surely he shall not be moved for ever: the righteous shall be in everlasting remembrance. He shall not be afraid of evil tidings: his heart is fixed, trusting in the Lord. His heart is established, he shall not be afraid . . .' (Ps. 112:6-8). Now, that is another way of saying that 'his leaf shall not wither'. A terrible drought may come, but the leaves of this tree shall not wither. Why? Because it is planted near the rivers of water. That river never dries up, and the roots and the tendrils of this tree are in that river-bed and drawing out of this river, never lacking in moisture. Let there be a terrible drought, still the moisture comes unseen and his leaf never withers.

This is one of the most glorious aspects of the Christian life. It prepares us for everything that can ever happen to us. It prepares us for middle age; it prepares us for old age. It prepares us for the days when we are decrepit and can scarcely move and scarcely think. It prepares us for illness; it prepares us for misfortune and loss. It prepares us for difficulties with other people. It prepares us for the death of loved ones. It prepares us for our own death. There is nothing that can happen to us but that this prepares us for it. I am planted by the side of the rivers of waters which can never fail, my life being in Christ. Psalm 92 says, 'They shall still bring forth fruit in old age; they shall be fat and flourishing' (v.14)—even in old age! God has promised, 'I will never leave thee, nor forsake thee', so that the Christian is able to say, 'The Lord is my helper, and I will not fear what man shall do unto me' (Heb. 13:5,6). 'Listen,' says David in Psalm 37, 'I have been young, and now am old; yet have I not seen the righteous forsaken . . .' (Ps. 37:25). 'Yes,' says the apostle Paul, 'I have learned, in whatsoever state I am, therewith to be content. I know both how to be abased, and I know how to abound . . . I can do all things through Christ which strengtheneth me' (Phil. 4:11-13).

> In heavenly love abiding,
>   No change my heart shall fear;
> And safe is such confiding,
>   For nothing changes here:
> The storm may roar without me,
>   My heart may low be laid;
> But God is round about me,
>   And can I be dismayed?
>   Anna Laetitia Waring

Of course I cannot! It is impossible. Let the storms come; let the hurricane arise; let the blizzard blow; let everything be let loose against me: it does not matter. 'I know whom I have believed, and am persuaded that he is able to keep that which I have committed unto him against that day' (2 Tim. 1:12). My life being rooted and grounded in Christ, I am able to say,

> Plenteous grace with Thee is found,
>   Grace to cover all my sin;
> Let the healing streams abound,
>   Make and keep me pure within.
> Thou of life the fountain art,
>   Freely let me take of Thee;
> Spring Thou up within my heart,
>   Rise to all eternity.

It does not matter where you are:

Jesus, lover of my soul,
  Let me to Thy bosom fly,
While the nearer waters roll,
  While the tempest still is high:
Hide me, O my Saviour, hide,
  Till the storm of life is past;
Safe into the haven guide;
  O receive my soul at last!
Charles Wesley

'His leaf also shall not wither.' Those who are planted in the house of our God shall flourish in the courts of our God.

Have you got this life? It is the only thing that matters. Are you planted in Christ? Are you living on him? Is he your bread, your water, your breath, your everything? Is he your all and in all? Are you ready for an unknown future? How are you standing up already to the trials of life? Is Christ sufficient for you? If he is not, you do not know him. If you are seeking any satisfaction apart from him, you do not really know him. 'Thou, O Christ, art all I want; More than all in Thee I find', says Charles Wesley again. And this is true, because his is the life of God. There is no end to it. He is the all-sufficient one. Oh, give yourself no rest nor peace until you really know him, until you know that you are in him.

Make certain that you are planted in him. If you are doubtful, plead with God. Tell him you want to be, and, do you know, if you do even that much, it is a proof that he has started dealing with you. You would not say that much if he had not started. He has been digging; he has been preparing; ask him to go on with the blessed work until you know that you are rooted and grounded in Christ. He said, 'I am come that they might have life, and . . . have it more abundantly.' Are you enjoying that more abundant life? It is all there for you in him. Make certain that you are planted in him. Then you will begin to bear your fruit in your season, and—most wonderful—your leaf will never wither, whatever may happen to you.

4
The two ways

*Therefore the ungodly shall not stand in the
judgment, nor sinners in the congregation of the
righteous. For the Lord knoweth the way of the
righteous: but the way of the ungodly shall perish.*
(Psalm 1:5-6)

These two verses come at the end of the psalm. They are
the conclusion, and in a sense they are also a climax.
What the Psalmist is doing here, as I have been showing, is to
teach us and to instruct us as to the one and only way in
which happiness or blessedness can be found. And the
method he has adopted is that of comparison and contrast.
Two men, two types of men, godly and ungodly; two ways
of life, the godly life and the sinful, or ungodly, life. And his
point is to show that the only hope of real, true happiness is
that we should be godly. Happiness, he says, depends ultimately upon our relationship to God, and upon what we are
as a consequence of that. But now, he comes to the climax,
and this, in and of itself, is something which is very characteristic of the Bible. The Bible always gives us a complete
statement, a whole view. The Bible never stops short; it never
leaves anything unfinished. If it sets out to deal with a case, it
tells you everything about it. And so, in these last two verses,
we find the Psalmist following what he has been saying.
'Therefore', he says, and follows it to its ultimate and inevitable logical conclusion.

He has been saying that true happiness is possible and that it is obtainable even in such a world as this. It is something that can be obtained immediately; it is not contingent upon other things; it depends upon one thing only. It is a happiness which lasts and which enables us to meet all eventualities and contingencies. We have considered all that. But now he goes further. It is a happiness, he tells us, that goes on for ever. It does not stop at this world; it goes on even into the next world. So, he tells us about the nature of the happiness, the continuation of the happiness in spite of everything, and the fact that it is an eternal happiness, a happiness that can even meet the last enemy and what lies beyond it, a happiness that goes on throughout the countless ages of eternity. And by contrast, of course, he has been telling us that the godless, worldly, sinful life, the chaff, is a very poor thing. It has no character, and is a complete contrast to the tree that he describes. And he tells us that it is never of any real value or profit to us—chaff that the wind blows away. But, and this is what he comes to in these last two verses, it is something that always leads finally and eventually to nothing but disaster. So we are concerned now only with this end, which he puts before us in these two verses. And I want to try to show you how this consideration of the end is that which makes the biblical message so unique. It is the thing that marks it off from every other kind of teaching that offers itself to the human race.

The end of life

Now the ultimate trouble with the man who is ungodly, or a sinner, or scornful, call him what you will—these terms are all used about him here and they are used elsewhere in the Bible—is, of course, that he is just a fool. He is a fool because he tends to live only for the present; he never looks ahead.

He is concerned about the happiness of the moment. He does not consider consequences or effects. He does not consider results. All he wants is what he can get now. The Bible has a term for all that: it calls it *inordinate*—'inordinate affection' (Col. 3:5). It cannot wait; it must have it *now*.

This is what the Bible tells us everywhere about sinners, that they are people who have this small view of life: present only, self-centred, selfish, small. And they refuse to go on to look at and to face the end of life. Not only do they not do that; even if you try to persuade them to do so, they argue against you; they dislike it and they dismiss it. They say that the thing to do is to live for the present. Why anticipate the future? It will be here soon enough. Why go and meet troubles? Live for the moment; enjoy yourself; let us eat, drink and be merry! That is the typical attitude, and it dislikes any suggestion or teaching that it should look ahead and consider what is going to happen, and what it is all leading to.

The tragedy of the ungodly is that they live from day to day, from hand to mouth, and think only of present satisfaction. And, even further, when you remind them of the fact that they are, after all, mortal and that they must needs come to an end, they say, 'It's all right, I'm not concerned about that, because when a man dies that is the end and there's no more to be said about it.' That is the modern attitude. It does not believe in the unseen or in the spiritual realm. It does not, in general, believe in a future life. This world only!

Now I say that people who hold this view are fools, because they have no proof at all for what they are saying. They cannot demonstrate anything. They cannot prove that this is the only life and the only world; they do not know. But in spite of their inability to demonstrate the correctness of what they are saying, they risk all upon a conjecture, upon a mere theory, upon a mere supposition. In a spirit of bravado they say that they do not care, and they are not prepared to listen. And there is only one word to use with respect to such people and it is that they are fools. The world does not like to face and to consider the future, but the Bible everywhere reasons with us and is always appealing to us to do so; exactly as this man does here in this first psalm.

The Bible, in other words, always emphasises the wholeness or the unity of life. The Bible says, 'Do not stop at considering your past and your present; anticipate the future, look ahead.' It never gives us a sort of piecemeal message. The world, of course, does that with its pleasures. It is not interested in your thinking ahead: have a good time *now*, have this enjoyment *now*; have this thing that appeals to you *now*. 'No, no,' says the Bible, 'look ahead; don't enjoy this until you've considered what it may lead to. Don't do anything until you've considered possible effects and results and consequences. Life', says the Bible, 'is a whole, and whether you like it or not, is a unity. It is past, present and future. It is youth, middle age, old age. It is being born, it is living, it is dying. There is a wholeness. Consider it all', says the Bible. 'Do not stop short at any point.' That is its first emphasis.

Death not the end

The second is this: the Bible proclaims that death is not the end. This is its message everywhere, right through both Old Testament and New: that this is only a temporary world; that we are only pilgrims and strangers here, journeymen, travellers; and that beyond this life and this world there is another, and we go on into that.

Indeed, in the third place, it always tells us that after death there is a judgment: 'the ungodly shall not stand in the judgment'. This is one of its great fundamental messages. Death is not the end; death leads to judgment; and, fourthly—and this is vital—our eternal destiny, our endless life in that spiritual realm to which we go when we leave this world, our destiny there, is determined by our life and our attitude in this world. What happens to us there is the inevitable, the logical, outcome of what we are here—what we think, what we believe and how we live. That is the point the Psalmist is making. There is this comparison between the godly and the ungodly, what they are, how they live, and so on; therefore, this is the end of it all. Here is the final contrast.

So this is the great central message of the Bible with respect to life, and what the Psalmist is saying can be put like this. The only man or woman who is truly blessed and happy, is the one who has catered for all and who is ready for all; the end, death and what lies beyond it, included.

That is the secret, says the Psalmist, of happiness and of blessedness. You cannot atomise life. You cannot divide it up into segments. You must take the whole. It is moving, something like a stream flowing along. And if you want to be really blessed and happy, he says, you must consider the end as well as the beginning. You must get the whole view. It is all one piece, and what is going to happen to you there, is determined by what you are here and now. This, then, is the Psalmist's message. The author of the Epistle to the Hebrews tells us of many people in this world who 'through fear of death were all their lifetime subject to bondage' (Heb. 2:15). Shakespeare agrees: 'dread of . . . the undiscover'd country, from whose bourn no traveller returns'. You cannot get true happiness in this world unless you have a faith that sees through death. It is impossible because, however happy you may be at this moment, you never know, there is always the threat, there is always the possibility, you cannot relax, as it were. 'All their lifetime subject to bondage.' That, says the Psalmist, is perfectly true; you must have a view of life that caters for the beginning and the end, all inclusive. And then, and then alone, are you truly blessed. 'Blessed is the man . . .' That is how he begins.

The fact of judgment

So, let us consider this matter of the end in three main propositions. The first thing which we must be clear about is the fact of judgment. 'Therefore, the ungodly shall not stand in the judgment.' Men and women are responsible beings, they are not animals—and, as responsible beings, they are held accountable and will have to give an account of themselves—the judgment. This message says that all men and women, everybody who has ever been into this world, will have to stand in a final judgment, a final assize. But, of course, the moment I say that, I know I am saying something which is utterly repellent to the modern man and woman and to the modern mind. 'Fancy still saying that!' people will say. 'Oh yes, a century or so ago preachers used to make great business with this judgment and used to frighten people into becoming religious. They terrified them, with thoughts of hell and punishment, into believing the gospel and into living a good and a godly life. But, of course, by now we know that this is all wrong. There's nothing in it, there's no such thing.' And their reason for saying that is this. 'You can't have it both ways', they say. 'If you believe in God at all; if you believe in a God of love, then judgment is something that is utterly incompatible with such a God and with such love.'

But all such objection to judgment is based, ultimately, upon completely false views of God and of the love of God. Let me just ask you a simple question: What do you really know about God? What right have you to postulate things about God? What right have you to say that if God is God and a God of love, he cannot at the same time be a just and a righteous God and that he cannot be a judge?

What do we really know about God? And the answer is that all we know about him is what he has been pleased to reveal concerning himself. And the only knowledge we have concerning God's revelation of himself is what we have in the Bible. Yes, you have it in nature. Thank God for it. I see his wisdom, I see his power, I see his design. But I can see God not only in nature, I can see him in history also. I see him in providence. But still, the God we know in those ways is an unknown God. Really to know the character of God we must come to this book. Here is the record of God's revelation of himself to men and women. The biblical writers do not say, 'This is what I think about God.' No: they say, 'God spoke to me; God gave me a revelation.' God called a man like Moses on top of Mount Sinai and began to speak and he said, 'This is truth, *I am*.'

We are entirely confined to the Bible, and, therefore, if you say you do not believe in a judgment because you cannot understand it and cannot reconcile it with what you think God's love is, then you are just basing your whole position on ignorance and upon speculation; upon what you hope; upon what you would like to believe. You have no basis for it at all. Over and against all this modern rejection of the notion of judgment stands the Bible itself, and if there is anything that is plain in the Bible, it is judgment. When God made Adam and Eve and put them in the garden, he said, 'Now if you break my laws I will exclude you from the garden.' And he did!

As I am never tired of pointing out, our world is as it is in sin because of God's judgment upon sin. He cursed the ground; he drove man out of paradise, and put the flaming sword and the cherubim to prevent his coming back. That is judgment in practice, in operation. The Old Testament is full of it. You get it in the case of individuals and in the case of the whole nation of Israel, even his own people. He sent them into the captivity of Babylon because of their sin. Judgment! He said he would do it and he did.

Then when you come to the New Testament you find the same thing. The first preacher who appears before us is John the Baptist. He preached a 'baptism of repentance for the remission of sins' (Luke 3:3), and as he addressed the congregation of Pharisees and scribes and others, he said, 'Who hath warned you to flee'—from what?—'from the wrath to come?' (Luke 3:7). That is the first note in the New Testament. Why is this a gospel of salvation? Why is it good news? There is only one reason: it is that it saves us from the judgment and the wrath to come. John the Baptist, the precursor, the forerunner, preached it.

But our Lord also preached it. The day is coming, he said, when all who are in the graves are going to rise, and they are going to rise to judgment (John 5:28-29). It will either be life or damnation. You talk about love! Does anybody know anything about love in comparison with the Son of God, our Lord and Saviour, Jesus Christ? He is the very incarnation of love. He has come into the world because God is love, because God so loved the world. And yet that is his teaching. Judgment! And it is one or the other. A judgment of damnation or a judgment which proclaims that we are the people of God and that we go on to everlasting bliss. It is in the teaching of all the apostles also. 'Save yourselves', says Peter, filled with the Holy Spirit on the day of Pentecost—the first sermon really, under the auspices of the Christian church—'Save yourselves from this untoward generation' (Acts 2:40).

The apostle Paul preached the same thing. Standing on Mars Hill in Athens, he said that God 'now commandeth all men everywhere to repent: because he hath appointed a day, in the which he will judge the world in righteousness by that man whom he hath ordained; whereof he hath given assurance unto all men, in that he hath raised him from the dead' (Acts 17:30-31). 'Listen', says the author of the Epistle to the Hebrews, 'We ought to give the more earnest heed to the things which we have heard, lest at any time we should let them slip.' Why? Well, 'How shall we escape, if we neglect so great salvation?' (Heb. 2:1,3). Escape! 'It is appointed unto men once to die,' he says later on, 'but after this the judgment' (Heb. 9:27). Peter agrees that the day of the Lord will come. It is bound to come. 'One day is with the Lord as a thousand years, and a thousand years as one day' (2 Pet. 3:8). But the day of the Lord will come. It must come. The Book of Revelation is but a preview of this ultimate, final judgment of the whole universe, the entire cosmos. That is the answer to all the modern objection. The fact of the judgment. It is the solemn fact which is held before us everywhere in the Bible. Do not follow the ungodly. Why? Because you must face that judgment.

The nature of judgment

Then the second principle is the character or the nature of the judgment. It is a judgment that takes place partly in this world. Sin produces a certain amount of punishment even here and now. That can be bad enough. 'The soul that sinneth, it shall die' (Ezek. 18:4). Yes, but 'the way of transgressors is hard' (Prov. 13:15). The sinner always gets into trouble. You cannot break God's laws and just go on as if nothing had happened. You have to pay for it: remorse; self-castigation; damage perhaps to your physical body; harm done to your faculties, God-given faculties. There is a judgment, a punishment even in this present world. But the great message of the Bible is, of course, to tell us that it is at the end that the judgment really comes. All these other things are but adumbrations of the judgment. Indeed, all the judgments in the Bible are but foreshadowings of the final judgment, preparing us for it; signposts, fingerposts, pointing to what is bound to come at the end of the age.

What, then, is its teaching? It is, to put it as simply as I can, that everybody will have to appear before God in the judgment. The whole world. Those who are still alive, those who have died, those who have been drowned in the sea, everything must give up its dead. The graves, the oceans, the elements, everywhere; and the dead shall rise.

We are also told that it is God's judgment. 'Therefore the ungodly shall not stand in the judgment . . . for the Lord knoweth the way of the righteous: but the way of the ungodly shall perish.' The judge is the Lord himself, 'The Judge of all the earth', as Abraham described him (Gen. 18:25). He is the judge because it is his world; because he made it and it belongs to him; because he set it going and because he has laid down the conditions. He is the judge, because he alone is just and righteous. He is judge, if I may put it with reverence, because he alone is fit to be judge and has the right to be so.

But our Lord has also taught us that the judgment has been committed to him because he is the Son of man, to make it yet more fair (John 5:22). Man might say, 'Ah, but what does God know about life lived by a man in this world?' The answer is, the Father has committed the judgment to the Son and the Son has become a man. 'The Word was made flesh' (John 1:14). The Son has lived in this world, has been 'tempted in all points like as we are' (Heb. 4:15). He understands and he knows all about it. He is the judge. The apostle Paul, as we have seen, taught the same in his sermon on Mars Hill in Athens (Acts 17:31). So the picture is of a day which is to come when the Son of God, the Lord Jesus Christ, will return to this world and will judge it in righteousness.

What are the terms of the judgment? They are made quite clear in the Bible. We shall be judged according to that which the Psalmist has talked so much about: 'the law of the Lord'. He tells us of the godly man that 'his delight is in the law of the Lord; and in his law doth he meditate day and night.' Now the law of the Lord is simply this: what God has said to men and women about themselves. It is what God has been pleased to tell them, in different ways and at different times, as to what he expects from them. God made them, and he has told them that he has made man in his own image and likeness (Gen. 1:26). That is the object and purpose of his creation. Men and women are to be a kind of reflection of God in the world. God has made everything, but he has made them a kind of under-lord; they are lords of creation under God.

Further, God, having made us, put certain laws into us and gave us certain laws outside, and he said, in effect, 'This is how I want you to live.' So, from time to time he has given us some very explicit statements of this law; and the clearest in the Old Testament is, of course, the Ten Commandments, which are but God's statement as to what he demands of us and what he will eventually and finally expect of us.

So we shall be judged by the Ten Commandments, and nobody need claim ignorance any longer, because God has put them before us. This is what he wants and that is how he will judge us. This is found in the teaching of the prophets who expounded this law. And then our Lord, in the New Testament, in the Sermon on the Mount, expounds it still more perfectly. The Sermon on the Mount is an exposition of

God's law. This is what God demands; this is what he expects. Our Lord has summed it all up like this: 'Thou shalt love the Lord thy God with all thy heart, and with all thy soul, and with all thy mind, and with all thy strength: this is the first commandment. And the second is like, namely this, Thou shalt love thy neighbour as thyself' (Mark 12:30-31). And we shall be judged by that law. 'Thou shalt have no other gods before me. Thou shalt not make unto thee any graven image . . . [and] bow down to them . . . Thou shalt not take the name of the Lord thy God in vain . . . Remember the sabbath day, to keep it holy . . . Honour thy father and thy mother. Thou shalt not kill. Thou shalt not commit adultery. Thou shalt not steal. Thou shalt not bear false witness . . . Thou shalt not covet thy neighbour's house, thou shalt not covet thy neighbour's wife . . . nor his ox, nor his ass . . .' (Exod. 20:3-17).

Those, then, are the terms of the judgment, especially as interpreted in a spiritual manner by our Lord himself in the Sermon on the Mount, which shows that it is not the actual deeds alone that matter, but the thoughts, the desires, the things we feel—God knows them all!

But what is emphasised here in particular by the Psalmist is what I might call the thoroughness of the judgment and of the gospel. 'The Lord knoweth the way of the righteous: but the way of the ungodly shall perish.' The Lord *knows*. He is omniscient. There is nothing that he does not know. There is nothing, says the author of the Epistle to the Hebrews, that is hidden from his sight, 'but all things are naked and opened unto the eyes of him with whom we have to do' (Heb. 4:13). The Lord knows. He is omnipresent: you cannot stand behind a shut door as far as God is concerned. It is impossible. The Bible teaches this in many different forms. The Psalmist complains, 'Thou knowest my downsitting and mine uprising, thou understandest my thought afar off' (Ps. 139:2). I cannot get away from you, he says. And the New Testament tells us that there are great books— it is a picture of great ledgers kept in heaven—and every one of us has a page in that ledger. Everything that each of us has ever done or thought or said is there recorded, written in the book; so that in the judgment the books are produced and everything is learned about us. Such is the thoroughness of the judgment. Nothing can be hidden from the sight of God. The very fact that God is God makes that inevitable, of course, but this is the thing that we forget. We are so clever at doing things in this world without one another knowing; we can deceive one another and we can lie and get out of it, and we rather admire the people who can get away with it. But nobody can do that with God. 'The Lord knoweth . . .' Nothing is hidden from his sight.

But there is another terrible way in which that is put here. 'Therefore the ungodly shall not stand in the judgment, nor sinners in the congregation of the righteous.' This is the most terrifying thing of all. If you take the similar use of this word 'congregation' as you find it in the Bible, you will find that it means exactly the same thing as the church. Or sometimes it stands for God's people. The congregation is God's own people, the church.

The Psalmist says here that sinners shall not stand in the congregation of the righteous. What he means is that while you and I are in this world, we can be in the congregation of the righteous. We can be members of Christian churches, and we can pass as godly and as Christian people. But what he is telling us is that, because God knows everything, it does not follow that we shall continue in the congregation of the righteous after the judgment, because God knows all about us. And there is going to be a terrible sifting and a terrible dividing. There will be a gathering, a congregation, and they all fondly imagine that they are God's people, and then he will come in the judgment and he will sift and divide.

Now, lest anybody may think this is just Old Testament teaching, let me give it to you in its New Testament garb, and out of the mouth of the Lord Jesus Christ himself, at the end of the Sermon on the Mount. He generally ends his sermons on a note of judgment and he puts it like this: 'Not everyone that saith unto me, Lord, Lord, shall enter into the kingdom of heaven; but he that doeth the will of my Father which is in heaven. Many will say to me in that day, Lord, Lord, have we not prophesied in thy name? and in thy name have cast out devils? and in thy name done many wonderful works? And then will I profess unto them, I never knew you: depart from me, ye that work iniquity' (Matt. 7:21-23). 'But, Lord,' they will say, 'haven't you been in our streets? We belong to the congregation.' But the word will come, 'I never knew you. You are not to stand in the congregation of the righteous; you do not belong to me, you never have done. You insinuated yourself amongst them; you wanted to get all the benefits. But God knows everything; I know everything. Go away!'

And as if that were not enough, our Lord spoke three parables on the same matter. You will find them in Matthew chapter 25. In chapter 24 he deals with the end of the world, the judgment, and somebody asks him, 'When is the end of the world coming?' He says, in effect, 'Do not worry about *when*, concentrate on what will happen when it does come.'

Then he spoke the three parables. The first is about ten virgins. Yes, but there is the same division as we have in our psalm: five were wise, five were foolish. But, they all appear to be the same: ten virgins. They all had lamps; they were all going to a wedding feast; there was no difference, you say.

But when the bridegroom came, there were only five in the congregation, and there were five hammering at the door trying to get in. But they were not given admission; they were outside, though they had thought they were all right. And the whole point of the parable is to teach the danger of thinking and assuming that you are in the congregation because you have a lamp and because you want to go to the feast. But they had no oil! none of that vital spirit of life. And they are outside.

The next parable is about three men and their talents. It is exactly the same point; and so it is with the last one, the final judgment of the nations, the sheep and the goats. The assumption was that they were all the same, but the whole point of the parable is to say, No! He will divide. Sheep and goats. Standing in the congregation of the righteous and not standing in the congregation of the righteous. Oh, the thoroughness of the judgment! We are dealing with one to whom all things are naked and open. The Lord knows. We are not dealing with human beings. We are dealing with the omniscient, almighty and everlasting God.

Consequences of judgment

And that brings me to my third and last principle, which is the consequences of the judgment. The fact of the judgment; the character and the nature of the judgment; and finally, the consequences of the judgment. And here it is in this graphic, tremendous phrase: 'Therefore the ungodly shall not stand in the judgment, nor sinners in the congregation of the righteous.' Let me put that into the colloquial language of today. What the Psalmist is saying is that the ungodly, in that final judgment, will not have a leg to stand on. That is how he put it. They will not stand in the judgment; their whole case is demolished. And that means that they will be speechless;

they will not have a word to say or a reply to offer.

What will be the charges? Well, here they are. *First,* they have never given God a thought. They lived as though there were no God. They had been made by God, for God's own pleasure, that they might glorify God and enjoy him for ever. But they had lived their lives as if there were no God. They had gone their own way, and if God were mentioned to them, they hated the thought. They did not love God. They were supposed to love him with the whole of their being, but they hated him and felt that he was against them, and they reviled the name of God. That is one thing.

Secondly, they had not lived to God's honour and glory. They had not kept the law of God and the commandments of God. Instead of delighting in the law of the Lord and making it their meditation day and night, they hated it, they cursed it, spat upon it and ridiculed it. They said, 'That is just keeping us down. I believe in self-expression. I do not believe in curbing myself—I let myself go. If I want something, I have a right to it.' They spurned the voice of God; they trampled on the decencies and the sanctities, and they gloried in that. They made beasts of themselves, and were proud of themselves as they did so. 'That is to be a man', they said, 'and not some namby-pamby miserable Christian.' That is the sort of thing that will face them.

And in the same way they will be examined and questioned as to their view of themselves; their view of humanity, their view of the soul. They lived in this world saying that human beings are nothing but reasoning animals. They did not believe in a special creation or that man was made in the image of God. 'Man', they said, 'is just an animal that evolved.' And thereby, of course, they were insulting their own nature, and insulting the God who made them, and they lived a life that corresponded to it, this life of chaff.

And as they stand there in the judgment and see the Son of Man; see the Son of God who became man and has shown us what manhood means, and what man is meant to be, they will be speechless. And then they will be examined with regard to the quality and the value of the life that they have lived. And they will see that it is utterly and entirely useless. A balance sheet will be struck; what is the end result of the things to which they have given themselves, the things for which they have lived, the things on which they have gloated, the things which they have enjoyed? What is the end result? What's the value? Chaff! Useless chaff!

But it will not stop at that; they will try now to justify themselves and to say, 'But I didn't know. I didn't realise!' And they are silenced again. They do not have a leg to stand on; there is no excuse. The knowledge has been given. The revelation is here; the Bible is full of it. God has spoken. There is no plea—ignorance of the law is no excuse. Here it is; people should make themselves acquainted with it, and God has made it plain in his Word, in his prophets, in his apostles and in his preachers. God is speaking to men and women warning them, telling them what he demands. There is no excuse. Ignorance is inexcusable because God has given the revelation.

But the *final* thing that will demolish these poor ungodl people, and leave them there, not standing and like a heap oi chaff in the judgment, is that they will be confronting the Son of God himself. If they turn to him and say, 'But the standard was too high; who could live like that? Who could love God with all his heart and mind and soul and strength, and his neighbour as himself? Who could live only to the glory of God and to his praise? Who could keep the Sermon on the Mount? Who could live the Ten Commandments? It's asking impossibilities; it's unfair'; then the answer will come back:

'Look at me. I left heaven and came into your world in order to save people like you. I came not to call the righteous, but sinners to repentance (Luke 5:32). My teaching was that they that are whole need not a physician; but they that are sick (Luke 5:31). The Son of man is come, I said, to seek and to save (Luke 19:10). And listen,' he will say, 'publicans and sinners heard me and came after me. Men and women who had fallen into sin to the very depth and dregs, they listened, they came, they believed. And here they are standing in the judgment; there is no excuse left.'

The final condemnation is that God's offer of free salvation in Christ Jesus was spurned and refused and despised. 'Therefore the ungodly shall not stand in the judgment'; they are demolished. But, alas, it does not stop at that. 'The way of the ungodly shall perish.' Finding themselves without a word of explanation and without a single plea, they will be sent into the 'outer darkness'—I am quoting our Lord's words (Matt. 8:12); to a place 'where their worm dieth not, and the fire is not quenched'—still his words (Mark 9:44); to a place where there is 'weeping and gnashing of teeth'—still the words of the Son of God (Matt. 8:12). 'The way of the ungodly shall perish'—'everlasting destruction from the presence of the Lord' (2 Thess. 1:9). That is the end for the life of the ungodly, the sinner, the scorner, the chaff that rejects God and his holy law and his Son.

Why is all this written? And the answer is that it is written because God is love. It is written to warn us while there is yet time; it is written to save us; it is written to show us that there is a way of deliverance, a way of escape. That is the whole message of the Christian gospel. That is why Christ, the Son of God, came into the world: because we are all by nature ungodly, we are all sinful, and if we die like that we will go to that destruction, to that everlasting punishment of hell.

But God has sent his message, and it is a message that calls us to repentance, to an acknowledgment and a confession of our sins. Repent and believe the gospel—that is the message; nothing else! See the blindness and the madness and the iniquity of it all. See the end to which it leads. Acknowledge it. Fall before God and confess it and admit you haven't a leg to stand on.

And then, believe his gospel, in and through his Son, our Lord and Saviour Jesus Christ. Here it is: 'Believe on the Lord Jesus Christ, and thou shalt be saved' (Acts 16:31). 'Now is the day of salvation' (2 Cor. 6:2). The door is not shut. There is no need to go to that end. Though all that we have seen is true of the ungodly, if they believe that Christ the Son of God came into the world to live and die and rise again for their reconciliation with God, immediately they are forgiven. They are received by God. They become children of God. They become like the tree. The Lord knows their ways and they will go on into the everlasting bliss and glory. That is the message. That is why this is written: to warn us, to call us to repent and to turn to God and to believe the gospel of his dear Son.

Have you believed all this? Have you seen the need of the coming of the Son of God into this world? Have you visualised the judgment? Will you be able to stand at that great day? If you have seen now, as you have never seen before, that you will not be able to stand, it is my great privilege to tell you, God still calls. Now is the day of salvation. Believe it and say with me,

> Jesus, Thy blood and righteousness
> My beauty is, my glorious dress;
> Midst flaming worlds, in these arrayed,
> With joy shall I lift up my head.

Bold shall I stand in that great day,
For who aught to my charge shall lay?
Fully absolved through Thee I am,
From sin and fear, from guilt and shame.
                                        Count Zinzendorf

Or in the words of Augustus Toplady:

When I soar through tracts unknown,
See Thee on Thy judgment throne;
Rock of Ages, cleft for me,
Let me hide myself in Thee.

Believe on this Lord, and then you will be able to believe the apostle Paul when he says, 'Who shall lay anything to the charge of God's elect? It is God that justifieth. Who is he that condemneth? It is Christ that died, yea rather, that is risen again, who is even at the right hand of God, who also maketh intercession for us' (Rom. 8:33-34). You are safe. No one can bring any charge against you. Believe on the Lord Jesus Christ and turn to him and say something like this—if you have never said it before:

O Christ, in Thee my soul hath found,
    And found in Thee alone,
The peace, the joy I sought so long,
    The bliss till now unknown.

I sighed for rest and happiness,
    I yearned for them, not Thee;
But while I passed my Saviour by,
    His love laid hold on me.

I tried the broken cisterns, Lord,
    But, ah, the waters failed!
Even as I stooped to drink, they fled,
    And mocked me as I wailed.

> *Now none but Christ can satisfy,*
>   *None other Name for me!*
> *There's love and life and lasting joy,*
>   *Lord Jesus, found in Thee.*
>
>   Anonymous

In Christ you need not fear the judgment:

> On Christ, the solid Rock, I stand;
> All other ground is sinking sand.
>   Edward Mote

You cannot stand on anything else in this world. You will not be able to stand in the judgment on anything else. Sinners shall not stand in the judgment; like the chaff they will be blown away. Are you standing on the Rock, Jesus Christ? Is he your only hope? Believe on him, and you shall be saved—now!